THE DIVINE SUCCESSION

The cover is a composition based upon Kandinsky's "Circles" (1934) and two reconstructed friezes of the Temple of Zeus at Olympia.

Alfred de Grazia

The Divine Succession

A Science of Gods Old and New

Metron Publications

ISBN: 978-1-60377-090-3
Library of Congress Catalogue Number: 2015917127
Copyright © Alfred de Grazia 1983, 2015
Second edition
All rights reserved
Metron Publications, P.O. Box 1205
Princeton, NJ 08540-1205

To

Earl S. Johnson,

melior magister myriadis

TABLE OF CONTENTS

FOREWORD

Plato could already say in ancient times "that when men first had thoughts about the gods, with regard to the way they came into being, their characters, and the kind of activities in which they engaged, what they said about these things was not an acceptable account of them or what well regulated men would approve..." *(Epinomis)* We should have to agree and add that the subsequent 2500 years have managed, also, to obscure the origins, characters and deeds of the gods.

Many philosophers have quit concerning themselves with religion, believing that the road to wisdom is paved with logical forms. I doubt, however, that they can evade St. Thomas Aquinas' medieval injunction, to wit, "The name of being wise is reserved to him alone, whose consideration is about the end of the universe, which end is also the beginning of the universe." (*Summa Contra Gentiles*, I,1).

In this book we take up the history of religion and consider the meaning of the universe. From the first, humanity had to be religious. It is still so. Further, it will be religious so long as it will exist. Religion is ultimately hope, and humans live on hope. So goes, in other words, much of my story. But to my surprise, I have discovered that there is really something to hope for. The two parts of my book, going from *theomachy* to *theotropy*, pursue a way from despair to new hope.

At all times every aspect of the human mind and behavior has been religiously affected. No bit of culture escapes religious relevance or effects. I mean this literally. Such is the cultural dimension of religion, which will be explained.

That religion penetrates the fullness of history and culture licenses us to draw upon any and all human settings for illustration and proof. Every person in every setting, no matter how secular, merits attention as religious man.

No trick is intended, no cunning definition of religion. Religion for us here is simply a belief in the existence of a metaphysical order, together with the practices relating to it.

The means that I employ to select, analyze, and report religious material will be recognized and approved by aficionados of scientific method. Not that the scientific method is used throughout; but, when I move off the frame of positivistic, empirical science, I execute the movement self-consciously, so that an ordinary reader, a scientist, or a philosopher of science will be alerted and recognize in the procedure a defined and denoted mode of thought. Once again, no trick in intended; all of my cards are on the table.

What will follow, then is a narration in two parts and three themes. These themes are: religion as delusion; religion as politics; and religion as truth. Although treated vaguely in this order, they are also intermingled throughout.

Under the topic of religion as delusion are carried the most important components of human nature and the most important historical transactions. We shall name and discuss these. Psychology, anthropology, and history are the conventional disciplines most heavily brought into play.

Under the topic of religion as politics, we survey the religious aspects of collective behavior, showing religion again to be the most important part of social behavior, with the disciplines of sociology, politics, and philosophy most sharply involved. Science can explain every aspect of religion, but paradoxically, it is religion in the end that determines the metes and bounds of science.

Under the topic of religion as truth, we move into metaphysics. All that historical man has attempted to achieve with religion is adequately describable by the scientific method. Most of it is also disposed of as anthropological material, not true religion. The residuum of true religion, which is also describable by scientific method, is not only considerable but also exists in its own right, functionally and eternally. This body of religion does not logically or essentially engage in controversy with science, nor with politics.

Religion is an autonomous human activity, a fact of existence, like a rock or a sexual discharge. It may be useful, but its utility is not its justification nor even ordinarily expected of it. We call this activity "divine," meaning simply a person acting truly religiously. Appreciating the immediate challenge that will arise at any claim to the word "truth," we hasten to ask for a postponement of its trial until more can be said about "truthful" activity. Few will object if, in the meanwhile, we define truth as an open question of religion; one need not fear being forced to his knees.

Part One

THEOMACHY

Man's moral record in religion is largely unacceptable, whether to humans or to gods, if such exist. No anthropologist, philosopher, or theologian is pleased with it. It has been continuously expurgated and in parts expunged, to make it look better than it is. To little avail. It still appears as total theomachy: a struggle of man against god, god against man, man against man in the name of gods, and man against his divine self.

Why should we be so unpleasant in regard to religion, most human of activities from primordial days to the present? The question sends us back to the beginnings of the human species, when religious behavior began. We seek to establish there, and thenceforth through the ages, the connection between religion and human nature, in mind and in practice, and to come to an understanding of the historical gods.

CHAPTER ONE

THE GENESIS OF RELIGION

To the fresh, mad eye of primeval man, the world was full of gods. The human mind worked so as immediately to create religion. It does so now and it did so at its beginning. This is a function common to all humans everywhere, at all times, intrinsic, inherited, irresistible. Religion is then naturally ecumenical; any two people anywhere can agree in general on what it is that they are talking about.

The mechanism is simple. The thousands of books, the infinite discussion over millions of fires, the pomp of parades, the grandeur of cathedrals, and the hysterical wars and killings about religion - all of this intimidates inquiry. Yet all of this, as we shall see, descends from the operation of the mechanism as if a holocaust would flare from a flint striking stone.

The human mind, as soon as it starts working, builds a multiple identity, a self-awareness. In the origins of the race, this trait is so pronounced as to set the creature apart from other forms of life. Self-awareness is the psychological manifestation of a physiology of the central nervous system, especially the cerebral cortex, which presents a person with the feeling of being at least two persons. It is like the bother of two eyes that cannot focus well upon a single object, but it is of course enormously more ramified and important.

Since the body is one alone, it is "intended" for one mind, one spring of action, a single commanding organ. Never mind that in some remotely related animals two brain centers occur, or, for that matter, that in man himself, there are such "lower" brain centers that have escaped the partition which we speak about here as self-awareness.

A person has the instinctive appreciation of and a nearly total apparatus for realization of unitary conduct. But this preparedness for the life of an ordinary mammal is rudely challenged by the sense of an inner conflict of selves, which can 'change one's mind' and redirect one's energies at any time, with seemingly little possibility of control. It delays by microseconds the instinctive response that the mammalian physiology and neurology crave.

The result of the perceived conflict, that "I am I, but who am I that says 'I am I'" is fear. We can call this fear existential because it is the absolute quality of human existence. The fear is indistinguishable physiologically from the anatomy and process of mammalian fear that arises out of non-existential causes; such would be the fear of a blow or of a lightning stroke. If it is to be distinguished at all from animal fear, existential fear has to be discovered by statistical means, by logical reasoning, by experiment, by psychiatric theory. We assume, hoping to be more empirical later on, that existential fear is a "free-floating" fear overload that characterizes the human and is attributable to the "fear of oneselves" associated with self-awareness.

This state of affairs called "self-awareness" is instinctively undesirable. Its advantages are ambiguous. It interferes with peace of mind; it blocks the instinctive action of the beast; it introduces unwanted self-consultation concerning decisions and evaluation of the effects of action. It introduces continuous distrust of the self. It requires, as will be amply discussed, an endless stream of devices and decisions, all basically intended to adjust the elements of the self to each other, some of them taking place within the bodily frame, others occurring in interpretations of and controls upon the outer world of other people and nature.

Obvious schemes occur to the human person. One is to stamp out the other selves, to produce a granite-like person unbothered by internal inquiries. Another is to kick out the other selves like unwanted children or undesirable tenants. The first method is workable only up to certain point; many subconscious activities occur and leak out onto external objects, no matter how impressive the monolith.

The second method, expulsion of internal conflicts, creates the human's world, but is not effective as intended, either. A lady who has a bad dream, and then doubles her contribution to a church collection, may successfully lower her level of anxiety, but is likely to receive more cordial solicitations from her church, which, if refused, may give her more bad dreams. A boy who perceives a ghost under his bed will in time flesh out the ghost with various traits, motives, and activities. Displacements of anxieties, that is, are boomerangs which, no matter how far flung, unerringly return.

Since the struggle of the selves is essentially psychological, it can be called supernatural. Then it is even more proper to call the projection and displacements of the self supernatural. To become more focused upon religion, it should be said that there is absolutely no resistance of the part of the human to displacing his internal world, in effect, living his life - upon super-sensory or ultra-sensory phenomena. It ill behooves the source to deny its essence in the world outside.

At the same time, the operation of tying a world of external supernatural phenomena to the world of internal supernatural phenomena is invariably expressed in ritual practices, that is, repeated related performances. The lady and the boy in the instances above establish practices. The ramifications of practice are limited both by the environmental forces governing practices and by the tendency to reiterate actions. From action to practice to habit to obsession goes the continuum, a rating scale on which, given the object in the world to which people relate, the same people can be graded, like churchgoers from once-in-a-great-while to those who would rather die than miss a church service. Paul Radin has properly pointed out "that all people are spontaneously religious at crises, that the markedly religious people are spontaneously religious on numerous other occasions as well, and that the intermittently and indifferently religious are secondarily religious on occasions not connected with crises at all."

"Fear made the first gods of the world," wrote the Roman Statius (c. 45 to 96 A. D.). In the long history of religion it is the only theory to come close to the truth. And man, in return, is theophobic, full of dread of god. The first gods were also the first humans, a scheme of delusions to map and control the immense, live universe. Everything seemed capable of turning into a god; hence gods were in everything (as the early philosopher Thales conjectured). They controlled everything, it appeared, but were unaccountable and did both the expected and the unexpected.

The simple mechanism of religion is then self-awareness, fear of the self, fears or anxieties displaced upon supernatural or tangible appearances of the world, and the development of practices to control and maintain transactions with the supernatural appearances. The drive to control oneself (oneselves, we should say) is paramount and moves man to wherever his fears alight. Again, Radin's anthropological surmise is acceptable: "man was in a state of fear, physically, economically, and psychically. Man thus postulated the supernatural in order primarily to validate his workaday reality." His aim was "the canalization of his fears and feelings and the validation of his compensation dreams."

The judgment of what is supernatural and what is tangible may bother intellectuals and theologians but has never been much of a problem to the ordinary person or priest. The logic of the multitude is foolproof: the supernatural is everywhere and is incorporated in tangible things. We shall come to understand science better when we appreciate the futility, yet inevitability, of its struggles to squeeze the supernatural out of the rocks and out of the mind. It is trying to make an animal out of man, just as the pesky theologians say, that is, trying to destroy all outward manifestations of the uniquely human person, if not the mind itself.

Mircea Eliade has reported well the state of mind of the "religious man" through the ages. (He uses the term as, for instance, H. D. Lasswell uses the term "political man," as the "pure" or obsessed type of actor in history.) Where we employ the term "supernatural," Eliade uses the term "sacred."

"For religious man," he writes, "the world always presents a supernatural valence, that is, it reveals a modality of the sacred." Every bit of the cosmos has its sacrality. "In a distant past" (but why not include today?) "all of man's organs and physiological experiences, as well as all his acts, had a religious meaning," "Homo *religiosus* always believes that there is an absolute reality, *the sacred,* which transcends this world but manifests itself in this world, thereby sanctifying it and making it real." "For religious man, nature is never only 'natural'; it is always fraught with a religious value."

Finally, "the sacred is equivalent to a power, and, in the last analysis, to *reality.* The sacred is saturated with *being...* Religious man deeply desires *to be,* to participate in *reality,* to be saturated with power. This rounds out an accord with our ides of religious genesis. Man naturally sees the world supernaturally. Reality is supernatural.

His heart and soul go into tying this reality to himself, to gain its powers. We should say that all of this grandiose ambition is to stabilize his mind, to let him live unanxiously, unfearfully, to be at peace with himself."

How good it is to be assured of this, too, as the Hebrew Elohim assures man, that he shall "fill the earth and subdue it; and have dominion over the fish of the sea and over the birds of the air and over every living thing that moves upon the earth," and that furthermore he has given him "every plant yielding seed which is upon the face of all the earth and every tree with seed in its fruit..." Elohim is thinking and working like any ideal reasonable man would think and work. All is divinely created, by hard labor. All is sacred, therefore.

Yet, granted that humans are bent upon creating the supernatural and tying it into themselves, why should they dispose of the credit to gods? Why should they not be frankly proud of the world that they create and control, whether it be supernatural of tangible? First there is the fearful fact that they do not control it. Second there is the fear that disregards fact. They fear that they may not control anything; man is born with an inferiority complex from not controlling himself. Third, there is the appearance of purposeful control of the world by non-humans, an appearance, one may insist, that has both invisible and perceptible substantiation.

Take up first the fearful fact that man does not control himself, or the world. Hence religion arises to drug mankind, according to Karl Marx: "religion is the moan of the oppressed creature, the heart of a heartless world, the sense of senseless conditions. It is the opium of the people."

Perhaps the most powerful suppressant of religion is the promise of science to give one such controls. "Serious" scientists do not pretend to such abilities or make such promises. On the other hand, they at least feel relieved when other "non-responsible" people, like science fiction writers or humanists or philosophers, make such claims in their name. "We are approaching the time when we will be able to control..." - and every human anxiety has its assurance - "our anxieties," "climate," "earthquakes," "approaching comets," "plague," "birth defects," "war," "governments," and ultimately "the challenge of death itself." This wealth of promises emerges from the instruments and procedures of scientific method, a process finding its way only through provably material entities.

For those who doubt the fulfilment of these promises, the outlooks of cynicism, stoicism, and pessimism - or, alternatively, religion - are available. A society dominated by the scientific outlook will, however, endeavor to persuade many of these of its promises, and for that will take over all of the trappings of propaganda and organized pressures developed over the ages by religions, and, later, political systems. The secular society is then in being.

However, there is still the fear that disregards fact. There is a factual element in anxiety, but additionally the aforementioned existential element. It is highly probable that no change in the human condition can erase this anxiety except the eradication of the human in man. Self-awareness can be detrained, stunned and doped, but never with complete success and never over a whole population for very long. If it could be done, it would long ago have been accomplished. We may suppose that most cultures, in one way or another, have tried to do so, with no lasting effect. Man has achieved every imaginably bad society except one of lasting soullessness.

But fear alone might bring forth the supernatural, and the ways of dealing with it, without gods, unless some inherent part of religious mechanism demanded them. For this we require both an internal and external cause. The divine being must be both in us and in nature.

The internal sequence may be suggested. If it is the plural self that disturbs our peace of mind, then the infinitely varied displacements of this self that are employed to ease the fears engendered by the civil strife of the ego are likely often to emanate as living forms. That is, the world created by the human mind is animated. The world is alive.

It is an absurd but common notion, fostered unfortunately by scientists who are disciplined observers trained precisely to observe objects as "stripped-down," that the human neatly undresses his thoughts of their libido before placing them upon the world. To the contrary, the human is naturally surprised, like the child bumping his head on a table, when whatever he encounters turns out to be unalive according to the battery of tests that his mind applies consequent to the encounter. "Everything is alive until proven dead" is the natural psychic principle to go along with "Everything is sacred, unless demonstrated to be secular."

To say then that a natural force has to be animated into a god by some separate superstition which the observer must be trained to apply is incorrect. Depending upon its impact, the force is a god or a manifestation thereof. It is historically, as well as psychologically, incorrect to think that humans invented gods as a kind of convenience to collect their thoughts and then gave them names. It is more likely that gods were observed and in the very process of perception named by ejaculations (so beginning human speech), and then, following natural observation, the world was ordered in consonance with the gods. As Hock well says about the early gods of Greece "... these gods were not felt by the Greeks to have been manufactured or invented as the 'Personification' implies; they were discovered and recognized, precisely as the modern scientist discovers and recognizes the effects of something that he calls 'electricity. '"

Furthermore, the apparitions of nature are anthropomorphized insofar as they seem purposeful and humanlike. The human, responding to a vast range of stimuli in time and space, entranced by the sky as well as the abyss, infiltrating his spirit into this vast world, is both psychologically and materially affected by them. It is practically impossible, for any length of time, to take the apparitions of the world impersonally.

There is "every reason" to regard the fall of a meteor as a purposeful intervention in one's life. It moves through the air like a flaming lance, sword, chariot, or torch held high. It is faster than a bird. It screams like a tiger. It strikes with the might of ten thousand men. As scientists say, "Everything must have a cause." Well, here the cause is a superhuman thunderbolter. From effects, one reasons to causes.

If especially there are periods of time when great effects are common and men are shaken by them, the gods are implied, even visualized, as when a comet resembles different human figures and organs. Men measure the effect carefully, as the ancient Etruscans every spot struck by lightning, to see in the measure of a divine intervention the intent of the god.

In summation, the age becomes confirmed as religious. The more intense, pervasive, and frequent the experiences, the more religious the age becomes. It is as certain as any other proposition of science, that, were an asteroid or comet of modest size to strike the globe, astronomy would promptly become astrology, meteorology divination, biology creationist, politics catastrophic, and theology revivalist. Evidence for this statement is strewn among all writings on the effects upon humans of close-in and crashing celestial bodies.

This divinity, perhaps the same, perhaps another, is known not only by celestial or other natural apparitions; it is also manifested in ways that will be demonstrated in chapter 3. The god is as prompt to appear as religion itself, inevitable in the primeval mind, as culture, too, is prompt to appear and as fast as it is instrumented, married into, if not born of, the sacred. We speak, thus, of a hologenesis of *homo sapiens,* culture, religion, and gods.

Logically, the evolutionary theory of a slow final development of *homo* is gone; so is the theory of cultural evolution, of the evolution of religions, and of the progressive evolution of a concept of god. All of these things are today very much perceived, afforded and functioning as they did in the first centuries of humankind.

The science that those of us who write books so highly esteem represents a sharp break with the history of mankind, but scarcely less of a break with the human thought and behavior of today. We can, and shall, make much of it, but should remember all the while that the proportion of science to religion in human behavior is like the ratio of the depth of the surface crust of the Earth to the radius of the whole globe, one to four hundred. And as the thickness of the crust varies beneath oceans and continents, so does the depth of penetration of the scientific method vary in different cultures and mind.

CHAPTER TWO

THE SUCCESSION OF GODS

The first god who was, remains in the latest god who is. The gods have been of the same descent, always, everywhere. I mean this not in the sense of many theologians, that, "Yes, God has been eternally Himself but we have gradually learned more about His nature," nor in the sense of many sectarians that, "Yes, people have forever worshiped false gods but gradually we are coming to see my God," but rather I mean it to say that the gods were discovered once, in the earliest times, and that there had been a direct descent of the same divinities down to the present. By "discovered" is meant that the first humans perceived gods in the world; they perceived the supernatural, and they took immediate steps to control it.

Such statements may provoke panic in various intellectual quarters, and we wonder whether to arrest the panic or let the room be cleared. Much of our religious thinking depends upon refusing or denying the statements. Even some hard-boiled anthropologists meekly purchase meliorism in religious history, part of the famous idea of evolutionary progress, some such belief as that by indistinguishable degrees, dull-witted savages become plant-worshipers, and these grow into deists, who later become monotheists and finally begin to be secularists - and anthropologists. Even those who do not believe in gods are quite sure that they are competent to distinguish good gods from bad ones.

Yet the history of religion permits the statement. Leroi-Gourhan believes that the Upper Paleolithic hunters were probably religious. I have supported this view in *Chaos and Creation* with illustrations of a probable mating of Heaven as a bison and Earth in the form of a woman. Much earlier practices respecting burials and the mounting of bear skull accord to Neanderthal man also basic religious ideas. Leroi-Gourhan (in *Religions de la Prehistoire*) produces a scenario of a large primordial religion from an "insignificant" incised tablet. What is revealed by relics must be only a token of full-scale rites of religion.

A recent Soviet excavation finds religious incisions on animal skulls hundreds of thousands of years ago; for that matter, Pietro Gaietto attributes sculptures to "hominids" of 1.5 million years of age; but, as I have argued in other works, the measurement of time is in a sorry state of disrepair. In *Homo Schizo I,* incidental to establishing the hologenesis of culture, a connection of symbols and the supernatural is made. In my general attempt there and elsewhere to shorten drastically the time of *homo sapiens* and to identify all discovered hominids as human, I am led logically to erase the need to account for a long period of stupid human development prior to a mutation, or natural selection, or social invention that would initiate religion, along with man.

Further, I am in accord with the claim of anthropologists Washburn and Moore, that mankind could have originated only once. It seems to me that humanity is so distinctive in its self-awareness and symbolism, and that these traits are so suffusive over the scope of human behavior, that, once human in these regards, thence human in all regards.

Paul Radin *(Primitive Religion)* argues against the belief, represented especially by Andrew Lang, Pinard de la Boullaye, and others, that the primordial religion contained a belief in a Supreme God or High God. Rather, "wherever a Supreme Deity or a High God... exists it is the belief either of a few individuals or of a special group." He is persuaded that ordinary people are bereft of sky religion, a thesis that is patently false and can only be precipitated out of the materialistic brew of early Marxist anthropology.

Our interest is not to enter this debate but to veer towards a more important truth. Earliest humans gave preeminence to sky gods, as soon as one or more might be discerned through the thinning canopy of clouds. Ouranos and his counterparts in other cultures were, as we have remarked, first Heaven, then God, corresponding to the canopy and the appearance of a great sun-like object (among many others) in the new skies. However, since we believe this tumultuous set of natural events took a part in creating the human race itself, we would maintain that man was never human before he was religious.

Some tribes appear to follow spiritualism and animism and lack astral heavenly gods of human quality. We find ancestral spirits and ghosts usually inhabiting territories and, if they are disembodied, lower parts of the atmosphere; or the atmosphere is a medium through which they may move more easily than by treading the earth. Indeed, was not the vault of heaven itself low? And was not the Earth the goddess, sufficient itself to the first age of religious awareness? The Clouds of Heaven were many and low, until they descended in deluges.

The Vault of Heaven was lifted and humans saw the heavenly bodies removing themselves to remoteness and, too, the gods and hosts of heaven behaving destructively and benevolently with their own wills and human features.

We can agree with Mircea Eliade (*The Quest: History and Meaning in Religion*) where, discussing Wilhelm Schmidt (*Ursprung der Gottesidee*) he says,

> It is true that the belief in High Gods seems to characterize the oldest cultures, but we also find there other religious elements. As far as we can reconstruct the remote past, it is safer to assume that religious life was from the very beginning rather complex, and that 'elevated' ideas coexisted with 'lower' forms of worship and belief.

Thus, a prominent, although not dominant school of thought in the history of religion, exemplified in the work of A. Lang, M. Muller, R. Pettazoni, W. Schmitt, and M. Eliade propounds the thesis that the first worshiper and hence the ancestors of all religions believed in sky-gods. We find their arguments persuasive and add to them what we know about actual prehistoric skies and catastrophic occurrences affecting the skies.

The belief in sky-gods is attested to both by the most ancient sources of religious practice and by the studies of modern so-called primitive peoples (whom we prefer to call "tribal"). All of the "great" religions begin their stories in the skies: The Judaic complex, the Greco-Roman complex, the Egyptian, the old Chinese religion of Heaven, the Meso-American complex, the Teutonic, the Persian, the Hindu. "The Chinese T'ien means at once the sky and the god of the sky." Among the less familiar religions, the Mongol, the Sumerian, the Babylonian, the Celtic, the Baltic, and the Slavic have nominated the sky and its god(s) for preeminence. Not only this; so far as one can tell, all primitive religions have important celestial referents, and we may quote cases from Eliade again:

> The supreme divinity of the Maori is named Iho; iho means elevated, high up. Uwoluwu, the supreme god of the Akposo Negroes, signifies what is on high, the upper regions. Among the Selk'nam of Tierra del Fuego God is called Dweller in the Sky or He Who is in the Sky. Puluga, the supreme being of the Andaman Islanders, dwells in the sky... The Sky God of the Yoruba of the Slave Coast in named Olorun, literally Owner of the Sky.

> The Samoyad worship Num, a god who dwells in the highest sky and whose name means sky. Among the Koryak, the supreme divinity is called the One on High, the Master of the High, He Who Exists. The Ainu know him as the Divine Chief of the Sky, the Sky God, the Divine Creator of the Worlds, but also as Kamui, that is, Sky. The list could be easily extended.

Why is the sky the seat of the gods and even the gods themselves? From his unmatched scholarship, Eliade fetches a proposition which we believe to be incorrect: "Simple contemplation of the celestial vault already provokes a religious experience. The sky shows itself to be infinite, transcendent... For the sky, *by its own mode of being,* reveals transcendence, force, eternity. It *exists absolutely* because it is *high, infinite, powerful."* This speculation which figures over several pages, stands without supporting evidence. It seems to say, "since heaven is divine, and the gods are celestial, there must be a reason; the reason is a) since the gods are there, the sky must have impressed man and b) the sky is impressive (for the gods are there)." The logic is confusing and borrows, though not with conscious purpose, the propaganda technique of showering agreeable statements upon the reader.

> Indeed, if one shows (as has been done in recent decades) that the religious lives of the most primitive peoples are in fact complex, that they cannot be reduced to 'animism,' 'totemism,' or even ancestor-worship, that they include visions of Supreme Beings with all the powers of an omnipotent Creator-God, then these evolutionist hypotheses which deny the primitive any approach to 'superior' hierophanies are nullified.

One must return to the beginning. Granting that the sky-gods and sky-religions are primordial, how is man prompted to perceive the supernatural there, place preeminent divine activities there, and make the sky the centerpiece of religion? If humans existed long before religion was invented, then it should be embarrassing to argue that the skies might exist for millions of years before the idea of religion popped into the minds of people everywhere (and very much the same idea of religion, that is, sky-religion without aeons of animism, pantheism, ghosts, totemism, and such other forms of religion).

Eliade does not explain how early religions would move from sky-gods to demonism, totemism and animism, and sometimes back, for modern tribes of this ilk meet no insuperable problem in adopting a sky religion such as Islam or Christianity. We offer two explanations. First, these religious practices were originally, have been, and are always with us, and are not at all embarrassed at co-existing with sky-gods.

The second explanation is consistent with the first. The sky-gods seem to have disappeared from many minds of our "high" civilization in favor of the worship of technology, cinema and political heroes, and a number of psychopathological quirks. "Primitive tribes," since explorers and anthropologists began their profuse reports, seem to have lost their sky-gods, too, or never to have had any, or to possess *dei otiosi*. May not these tribal people be acting like these civilized people in focusing upon the sky-gods when the gods are active, or when the memory of them, consciously or unconsciously, is acute, tending to dismiss, forget, and deny them when they are not causing great trouble? The skies became peaceful and the world stopped shaking; people turned to the supernatural manifestations of their closer environment. In this case, we may surmise also that the sterner the institutions of memory (records, graphics, priesthoods, bureaucratic churches, holidays) the longer the sky-gods will persist in a culture.

Faced with embarrassment, the idea of long evolution of religion (but then perhaps, too, of the long evolution of man) might be dropped. Then at least, we see man becoming human and sky-religious concurrently.

But another embarrassment occurs. If this occurs at one place and one time, as we have asserted, how do all people settle upon the sky and often the same creation stories of first generation gods, as we shall see? "Diffusion," one might venture; from the first Adam and his home locale, there went forth the common focus and story (" Just as the Hebrew *Genesis* says!"?). If so, the first human must have achieved the diffusion; there would be no humans to pick up the story elsewhere.

In his book of *Timaeus,* Plato accepts and rationalizes in its early pages the existence of "everything visible, and which was not in a state of rest, but moving with confusion and disorder" prior to the work of the *Divinity* or *demiurge* which in its plenitude of intelligence and power "reduced it from this wild inordination into order."

Here is the first revolution; a Chaos, worked upon by a Demiurge (God) produces Order. This is a common ancient myth but we recall that Timaeus is a highly sophisticated Pythagorean and thinker. I conclude that the first of all great events remembered by man and emplaceable in primevalogy is the separation of Heaven from Earth.

The Divinity, according to Plato-Timaeus, using earth, fire, water, and air from the universe formed (generated) it into a figure, an animal containing all figures and animals and gave it the 'most becoming'... "spherical shape, in which all the radii from the middle are equally distant from the bounding extremities." So says Taylor in his great commentary on *Timaeus.* This universe moves in a circular revolution.

Taylor concludes that the boundless, the universe before god was composed of thick cloud or mist to early and late Greek philosophers. Fire made it visible and that is why it became the first of the elements.

There is a major dilemma in *Timaeus,* faced by all philosophers and theologians who explain creation. Was God always around but disinclined to do anything about the Chaos? Then finally did he act and make order, i. e., the universe as man knows it?

My interpretation is as follows:

The Cosmologist is Man.

Man senses ancient experiences.

He asks *when* did experience begin. In fact, he is asking "when did I begin?" i. e. my inquiring mind.

He thinks everything always was, because this is a logical thought.

He recollects, however, a time before the time he recalls, and remembers such time as chaos or disorder (or thick fog).

This time of the ordering of chaos must be either a memory of when man first got his head straight, i. e. could reason and ask basic questions, or an actual revolution of his nature or environment (a catastrophic set of events involving perhaps the lifting of a low canopy from Earth) which he recalls because he was already homo sapiens in all or part; but *he* cannot recall any *specific* catastrophic events before this time; therefore it becomes his creation moment, his gestalt of creation.

Then there are later stories about divine and celestial behavior that are found throughout the world, as, for example, the later coming of an electric or thunderbolting god. For instance, Eliade comments, as have I, on "the later transformations of sky gods into storm gods." Is this diffusion, or a common experience of separated people? Evidently, religious historians do not sense that a sequence of gods might exist, which are related to real natural events as experienced by widely separated people, such events being originally involved in the selection of the sky as the first god and the home site of the gods.

Religion begins and endures in the sky, and the gods with it, because the sky has been much more than the sky that we experience today. The oldest religions and tribal legends agree generally that the skies were a heavy and full covering of the Earth, that they became turbulent, descending upon the Earth, that they broke and discharged liquids and solids upon the world, that before man's eyes the god of the sky took shape, and that here was the first or Ouranian religion.

The primordial heaven and god do not endure forever. And at this point, Eliade recalls the famous ancient concept of the *deus otiosus*, the distant, removed, hence disoccupied god. Having created the world, the first gods generally retire. "Celestially structured supreme beings tend to disappear from the practice of religion, from cult; they depart from among men, withdraw to the sky, and become remote, inactive gods *(dei otiosi);"* Eliade presents relevant cases. "Everywhere in these primitive religions, the celestial supreme being appears to have lost *religious currency.* . . Yet he is remembered and entreated as the last resort. . ." A quantavolutionary would surmise that the tribal (' primitive') response to a long period of settled skies is exactly like the civilized society's response: to forget in part the great gods of disastrous ages, to secularize, to reduce religion to superstition, and also to make the Sun a catch-all for the gods.

But once again Eliade resorts to reductionist explanation and writes such lines as, "The divine remoteness actually expresses man's increasing interest in his own religious, cultural, and economic discoveries." He illustrates the "remoteness" by cases where in good times, gods are ignored, only to be appealed to in desperate times. This is a very different remoteness. In the celestial archetype, god is remote because he is not around and operative; in the second case, god is present but neglected.

Eliade does not bring out the most striking fact about the retired god. His is often a forced retirement, following a bloody, world-shaking revolution. The Greek Ouranos was castrated by his son Kronos in a terrible revolt, and moved into exile, with no intimations of a return to power. A new great age begins.

The birth of the great goddess Athena is reported in the Homeric "Hymn to Athene."

> Athene sprang quickly from the immortal head and stood before Zeus who holds the aegis, shaking a sharp spear: great Olympus began to reel horribly at the might of the bright-eyed goddess, and earth round about cried fearfully, and the sea was moved and tossed with dark waves, while foam burst forth suddenly: the bright son of Hyperion stopped his swift-footed horses a long while, until the maiden Pallas Athene had stripped the heavenly armor from her immortal shoulders.

Moreover, the new great gods are also celestial. They are not household familiars, woods sprites, or volcano ghosts. The Greek pantheon is well-known, but there are others as well. All of the great Greek gods are sky gods, though they may keep house on Earth as well, Hephaistos on Lemnos, Hades in the nether regions, and so on. The great ones are identified with the moon and planets: Aphrodite, Kronos, Zeus, Hermes, Athena, Ares, and possibly Apollo, Uranus, and Poseidon. (We do not refer, of course, to contemporary nomenclature.) When these gods are entered upon the historical record, dim though this time be, a period of greatest power can be assigned to each; this project was undertaken in *Chaos and Creation*. Then the sequence goes: Ouranos, Aphrodite as Moon, Kronos, Zeus (Hera), Apollo, Hermes, Athene and Hephaistos as Venus, and Ares. And there is substantial reason (not commonsensical) that these gods achieved power, fame, and worship because they were identified with great sky bodies, such as the planets, upon the occasion of great natural catastrophes befalling the Earth.

Scanning Samuel Kramer's collection of *Mythologies* of the Ancient World, we find persistent outcroppings of the procession of gods and ages despite his complete disregard of events in the heavens that might differ from the behavior of the sun, moon, planets, comets, and stars today. We find dual splitting creation gods, of the type of Earth and Ouranos; we identify Saturn, Zeus, Venus, and Mars, and also stories of cataclysms of the raising of the sky, and of world ages.

In the *Epinomis*, Plato is accomplishing a significant trick of theology. Complaining of the mythology that places the gods on Mount Olympus, he replaces them upon the planets where, he says, they belong, hoping to reform their bawdy characters thereby. He says we must get rid of any notion of the strife of the gods. They move always in order. (Elsewhere, Plato would have any disbelievers in orderly skies punishable.) The astral gods are the real ones, he insists, and gives them their names. (He anthropomorphizes the vault of Heaven, Kosmos.) Their names, he suggests, should be coordinated with Syrian and Egyptian observations, which are much older and "tested by vast periods of time." To us it occurs that bringing the gods down to Olympus was psychologically an effort on the part of Greek myth-makers to control the gods; they became human and tied to human fortunes directly. Now Plato, feeling no threat of planetary disorders, wants to send them back to their former homes, which are once again safe. *Dei otiosi,* the removed gods, will be doubly safe, safe for themselves and safe for mankind.

We note that the Greek and many other cultures regard their sky gods as blood-related. To the Greeks - to us, for that matter - this could only mean that their history was intertwined, overlapping, of the same order of celestial experiences.

We note further that the greatest Greek philosophers and scientists did not argue against the succession of gods. They did not challenge the succession, because somehow it was real to them. Somehow they were experientially or psychologically inhibited from claiming that the gods were born together. And so it was with other great ancient mythologies.

Eliade hardly pries into the secrets of the Hebrew gods; yet, guided by the hypothesis that gods occur in succession, and lend their new traits to religion, it is not difficult to see in the Bible and the legends of the Jews a series of gods, not badly matched with the Greek and Mesopotamian gods. These were objects of worship by hostile factions. At the least monotheism becomes, if not polytheism, then serial polytheism. Thus, in the opening passages of *Genesis,* the figures of Ouranos and Kronos are vaguely discernible, occurring in turn, whereupon intimations of worship of the Moon, Jupiter,

Hermes, and Baal-Venus intrude. The Archangel Gabriel, through Jewish legend, can be linked to the planet Mars, and the destruction of the Assyrian army of Sennacherib in 687 B. C. Yahweh, who is linked to Elohim (Saturn-Kronos) by Mosaic fiat, seems to be a Zeus-Horus-Jupiter figure to most scholars, and seems also to be a Thoth-Hermes-Mercury figure, blended with the Zeus figure, to the present writer (see *God's Fire: Moses and the Management of Exodus*). This latter god(s) can be fitted into history at the beginning of the Old Bronze Age in Egypt and the Near East.

Thus, there has been a succession of gods and goddesses in human history. Yet human nature is obsessive, that is, faithful; further, it was a great sacrilege to forget god, and severe punishment and expiation not only followed forgetting but were performed as prophylaxis. The compelling reason to change gods is to be found in reality. The reality is that the gods have changed, and, despite all his efforts to be loyal, man has been forced to worship new gods over the ages.

The ambivalence of the gods caused mankind from the beginning to exert itself strenuously to control them. A continuous redefinition occurred. Yet never has the nuclear complex of a god been put aside without great external pressures, the most excruciating of which has been the advent of an apparently more flexible and potent deity. In these cases, people have, as often as they could, tried to merge the new and the old; any evidence of continuity and any confusion of identities, whether physically or psychologically produced, have been seized upon to establish that the worship of the new is faithful to the worship of the old.

Therefore it happens, consciously or not, that all gods have an unbroken line of ancestors going back to primordial chaos; there the gods are made from the abstract elements such as air and water or the world begins out of nothing. We should bear in mind that when Egyptian history opened, with the Pyramid texts, Osiris (Saturn) was already dead, *deus otiosus,* and Horus (Zeus) reigned. Thus too, recorded history and ruins of civilized settlements portray the Saturnian (Osirian) "Golden Age" and its horrendous destruction.

The god Nun of Egypt, first god of the first recorded cosmogony, bears in his hieroglyphic name that he is of the primordial wastes of water in the sky, and Egyptian legends state this to be the case. Mother Earth, *Terra Mater,* the Universal Genitrix, Gaia, is the most durable of the gods, and found practically everywhere. In Hesiod's *Theogony*, she gives birth to Ouranos who is "a being equal to herself, able to cover her completely." It is clear, however, that Earth (who may even be conceived of as masculine sometimes) reacts to the changing gods of the skies, even when given a role in the celestial dramas of change. This Nun or heaven is "father of the gods," and father of Atum or Re. He or it is the demiurge of the boundless, featureless darkness, from which evolved the first hills or eminences. There appeared in early Egypt four different cult centers with special creation myths, all of which were essentially the same.

In Sumer in the 5th millennium before the present, as legend has it, Nammu, whose ideogram carries the meaning of "sea," was called the mother of heaven and earth who also bore the gods. Fluids and gases are favored elements of chaos and materials of creation. There is more than a semblance of logic alone in this accord of legends; the idea that gases go with chaos is attractive but is more than *ex post facto* explaining of legendary fiction. Fluids and gases must indeed have enveloped primordial man and attended the birth of the gods. Ouranos emerged out of the watery and turbulent wastes of the sky cloaked in robes of clouds. Philo Byblius anciently reported from earlier sources that the first Phoenician god was Elium or Hypsistos (" the Highest") and was succeeded by Ouranos who was succeeded by El or Kronos. But I would interpret this primordial god as the first stage of Ouranos, the adamantine condition of the sky prior to its breaking open to reveal the great light of Ouranos.

The Babylonians, successors to Sumer, in the early third millennium B. C., worshiped Marduk-Bel (Baal) as patron god and world creator, exalted over the old Mesopotamian pantheon just as Jupiter came to be exalted over Saturn in the Roman-Greek pantheon. Poseidon (brother of Zeus and son of Chronos) remained in heaven after his father fell and only later, upon agreement with Zeus, descended to rule the seas. He also flooded the land as he did so and was known as the land-encroacher. Thus the descent of Poseidon (Neptune) is to be identified with a great deluge, perhaps a name for, it not a later part of, the same great deluge that is connected with the crippling and binding of Kronos (Saturn) and is the same as the flood of Noah brought down by Elohim in Hebrew *Genesis*.

The qualities of new gods were thus to replace, overlap, and add to the qualities of the old; theology assisted by political power and the manifest abilities of the new god performed the task. Jupiter, for example, was called "fecundator," but the original fertilizer of the Earth and founder of agriculture was his father, "Saturn fecundator." The process by which the Sun usurped the identity and history of the old gods over the past two thousand years is homologous; when the skies settled down, this great and apparent sky-body grew in religious stature.

Buddhism climbed upon Hinduism; Confucianism and Taoism evolved from the worship of T'ien. The Christians and Muslim supplied "new testaments" to the Hebrew "Old Testament." There are no "Great Religions" in the world whose occurrence cannot be contemporaneously connected with natural events of the caliber of world-wide catastrophe. The same applies to small but persistent, durable religions such as modern Judaism, and Parsiism, descended from Persian Mazdaism through Zoroaster. I do not speak of many other religions of the world, some of which may well be "superior" or more deserving of the title "great" by such criteria as may be advanced in discussion. Nor do I distinguish among sects within the "Great Religions," while recognizing that in reality there may exist distinctions as significant, say, among Christian groups as between the "average" Christian religion and other religions. We hear of many instances in which Christians or Muslims are more comfortable among "head-hunting" sects or gnostic or totemistic religion than among their own kind.

An important line of attack may be leveled against our assertion that the succession of gods reflects a series of natural catastrophes upon Earth. Religions have continued to acquire new gods without actual catastrophes and have spread widely without catastrophes to help them do so. Some of these religions have been militarily aggressive, others peaceful. Thus Islam conquered large areas at first by the sword, as is well known, but in recent decades has converted peoples readily with little bloodshed and compulsion, as in central Africa. Farther back in time, as Wheatley (The *Pivot of the Four Quarters*) asserts, the Hindu pantheon moved into Southeast Asia along with its social institutions. Along with the religion went peaceful commerce. Many shrines were erected, around which there grew up cities. So enthusiastic were people for the peacefully inculcated religion that sometimes the near totality of a state's economy was given over to oblations to the pantheon.

The 2600 years since the probable last great natural catastrophes have not been distinguished by peacefulness. War and slaughter have been conducted in the name of a warlike religion (or interpretation thereof), or of a peaceful religion, or in the name of no religion but the state or tribe. We are led, then, to conjecture that *homo sapiens* himself, though relieved of direct models of destructive behavior in the skies, continues to carry out deeply rooted impulses to destruction, whether through unconscious memory or because he is constructed genetically to do so. That both are in fact the case is a main thesis of my two volumes on *Homo Schizo*.

So long as the skies were disturbed, and the Earth with it, the character of religion reflected clearly natural events and imposed models of conduct upon man. But religion itself was born in the creation of man and, if he were other than true to his nature or were of another nature, he would not have a peaceful religion and behave peacefully in all probability. Religion is a dependent variable of human nature. It is a dependent variable of natural events. We shall have to inquire, as we proceed, whether, in some other sense, in another kind of reality, religion may be an independent variable, owing its existence to conditions freed of human nature and ancient natural disasters.

To speak of religion as a variable reminds us of how vague and intangible are the materials of the history of religion and even of religious behavior today. We must toy with notions of impractical super-surveys, in frustration over this situation.

To speak properly about the religion of a person, a standard intensive interview at the least is required. "What precisely are your perceptions of the supernatural?" "What practices, life-pattern, or habits do you possess that are related to these perceptions?"

Then, of course, inasmuch as one's behavior is never quite aligned with one's professed beliefs and behavior, one should bring in some external objective testimony to supplement the interview. We should have hundreds of pages per person, but only from these would we be able to define operationally the person's religion.

Were all the people on Earth thus interviewed, and the results properly classified, tabulated, and analyzed, we should be able better to generalize about the relation of present religion and gods to the historical religions and gods - provided, we should add, that we have assembled and ordered all that might be known about historical religions back to their origins in the origins of man; this, however, we should probably be incapable of doing unless we were to adopt as the guiding hypotheses those already suggested in these first chapters: namely:

The earliest human cultures were simultaneously religious.

The earliest and most important supernatural objects everywhere were celestial.

The Ouranian complex of Heaven and Gods was the first list of *Dramatis Personae* of religion everywhere.

The Ouranian complex was overthrown by nature and simultaneously by man.

All successive gods everywhere have descended from and relate to the Ouranian complex.

Man believed himself forced to change gods from time to time by evidence in nature.

Man, as he changed gods, accomplished the transition with as few variations as possible in previously assigned powers, traits, names, vestments, rites and religious conceptions.

In these transitions, man became adept (to his way of thinking, which was and is delusory) at reconciling and controlling his gods through his religion, whence, by controlling the gods, at controlling the world, all with the ultimate and impossible goal of obtaining self-control and peace of mind.

CHAPTER THREE

KNOWING THE GODS

The collected qualities of gods resemble a bazaar where all types of potentially useful objects, frequently queer, are brought in by all sorts of people. The childish, outlandish and genial effects of the human mind are displayed in seller and buyer alike.

What brings one to the market: curiosity? hope of a rare beautiful utensil that one can afford? something to lighten our spirits? the euphoria of the busy scene? a thing - we know not what - that may change one's life? So one shops for gods. Some say, they are in everything. Some say, you cannot find what don't exist. Some say, they are most useful. Others say, they are not to be found when you need them.

If it were not for the fact that two billion people claim to know one or another god, perhaps we should scarcely bother to take up the question of what is known in this regard. Further, since most believers claim that their god wishes to be adored, and is infinitely capacitated, should not the god display himself clearly and prove at least his own existence, if not his other qualities, beyond a shadow of a doubt? But he avoids the flea market. He seems to want privacy, but then he should certainly resent the continuous universal efforts to bribe him to appear.

A few hardy souls venture to say that gods have little interest in humans and therefore have no motive to prove themselves. Some, like the deists, argue that the gods created everything and set it into motion; then, retiring, the gods left the world to develop by itself. Some merely say: "God works in mysterious ways his wonders to perform." (There is, incidentally, a religious adage for every circumstance.) Most who believe in gods - these are in numbers largely of the Hebraic complex or Hinduism - prove their case by pointing to divine signs (hierophanies), including the marvelously intricate reality of the world, by asserting there must be a purpose to everything, and by commanding, "Don't ask questions; have faith."

Gods appear directly to people, especially to heroes, on occasion; if not the gods themselves, then surrogates or messengers reveal themselves, if not these, then hierophanies or manifestations of gods occur. Dozens of gods, thousands of agents and subordinate gods, and tens of thousands of hierophanies, performing in plural appearances, would, if catalogued, constitute millions of appearances. Zeus knew many women; Athena marched before many soldiers; Buddha came from a noble family; Jesus was known among the people as a man; Paul met him on the Road to Damascus, resurrected; children of Fatima conversed with Mary, Mother of Jesus.

Millions of such encounters have gone unreported because of the modesty of people; they could not believe their good luck. In some religious sects, it is expected that now, if not earlier or later, every member must experience at the least a significant hierophany and a changed life thereafter.

A divine appearance or hierophany must be social, not individual, in the sense that it must the authenticated by the belief of others. This has not prevented millions of individuals, at some risk of persecution, whether criminal or medical, from claiming encounters.

Who validates encounters? This is properly a subject for the political science of religion. Who "should" validate them is the claim of as many theistic religions as exist. A large bureaucratic church may devote much energy to acknowledge any encounters, sometimes saying that god does not conduct himself so, or that he did once but now does not.

All sects lay down (that is, their gods lay down) rules for encounters. It is unthinkable that a Christian could conceive of his god going about raping women as Zeus was inclined to do. On the other hand, Yahweh, the god of Moses, delighted in the killing of enemies both foreign and domestic; at least so says Moses in numerous cases, as when the heresy of the Golden Calf is discovered, and the Lord's order is "slay every man his brother, and every man his companion, and every man his neighbor." Three thousand Israelites were killed that day.

In the Hebraic complex, Moses is the central figure. "Moses spoke with God." These conversations have been subjected to analysis for thousands of years and it is unlikely that late psychiatric explanations such as have been offered by Julian Jaynes and the present author will be final. Be that as it may, the relationship of Moses and Yahweh can be analyzed within the framework and propositions of the psychology of hallucinations and delusions. That is, Moses was conducting interior psychological operations. Yahweh was, to his mind, a real sacred Lord God.

By treating the world around him - the Egyptians, the Israelites, the desert, the architecture of sacred enclosures, the bushes, rocks and waters, and his disciples as if they too were under the direction of Yahweh, Moses created a marvelously integrated religious complex recomposing this world and himself in the midst of great natural turbulence. The more one studies the Books of Moses, the more sense one can make of them as literal history written by a deluded and masterful genius. But this hardly advances the cause of the Hebraic religions.

Increasingly, psychiatry and physics are pressing upon religions to surrender all cases of alleged hierophanies. The majority are easy to prove false. But, as we shall see later on, science is "getting too smart for its own good," and beginning itself to present important arguments concerning the supernatural - its own hierophanies perhaps.

Certain types of ancient hierophanies lend themselves to scientific reinterpretation. Examples are the collectively witnessed catastrophes of great magnitude - such as the Deluge of Noah - and electrical discharges of types no longer experienced, such as were central to the operations of Moses' Ark and the Delphic Oracle. Whereas new evidence and scientific interpretation go to prove the veracity of ancient reports, the supernatural character of the reports is thrown into doubt. Thus, a substantial proportion of the appearances of Yahweh in the *Books of Moses* occur in connection with (literally "on") the Ark of Moses; most probably these were electrical displays, ingeniously managed, and believed to represent the fiery essence of the deity.

Deluge legends are worldwide. Survivors included not only Noah's family but, to believe their legends, other people in different places on Earth. Evidence of large-scale flooding, totally beyond present experience, is worldwide. The cause, focusing now only upon the floods contemporary with Noah, were exoterrestrial and the water was in large part new water from outer space, maybe from a nova of a theretofore much larger Saturn. The establishment of this theory, even if it is accepted as the second most likely alternative to "no worldwide flood at all," reduces the religious and hierophanic aspects of the Hebrew story (and of all other religious descriptions).

Those who before saw the direct intervention of an explaining, instructing, humanly motivated god in the deluges gain a minor victory from the validation of sacred scriptures, but suffer a defeat of the notion of a divinely chosen people working under the immediate personal direction of their god. Dozens of peoples, perhaps all of them, inherit the belief that the gods once saved only them from a worldwide ruin. Doubt is cast upon all ethnocentric religious aspects of the Deluge, whence some persons will be led to a "higher religious synthesis" of the relations between gods and the natural world, while others will be led out of religion entirely.

Many people believe that they know gods by their effects, not by the grand effects of nature but by targeted effects upon issues of personal concern. The word "god" in Aryan etymology stems from the words "to sacrifice" and "to invoke." Invocation, prayer, and rituals are seen to be followed by events unexplainable except by a direct divine intervention. A sick child is for example, the object of medical therapy and religious solicitations; a cure is accredited to the divine; a failure of cure may be deemed to be in part a punishment, or the result of unconvincing solicitations. Seeking divine attention and determining whether and how it was provided take altogether too many forms, most of them well-known, to consider them at length here. The scientist will say "Explain all effects by natural causes; those not precisely determinable must be natural as well; where psychological effects are produced, these too are natural; for the human mind and its morale can be significant producers of effects in the context of human activity."

Modern theologians and religious practitioners tend to transmogrify all forms of knowing about gods that seem vulnerable to the lances of science. Most theology has been apology for vulgar religion. Realizing, for instance, that mental asylums are well populated by hallucinators, they are most approving of more subtle religious encounters. Encounters are favored that do not implicate divine personages or voices or external visions, but which display simple faith, spiritual resources, and the Lord secondhand. Thus, "I have faith in a benign Intelligence. It enables me to draw upon deep spiritual resources. I feel like Jeremiah, when the Lord told him 'Behold, I have put my words in your mouth. '" The problem of hallucination ceases as soon as one uses indirect quotation, "I think that god would help me to defeat the enemies of our country." This technique works all the better because in a bureaucratized society it has become rather insane for any job-holder to say "I" do this or that, rather than "We" or "our policy" or "the management" or "they."

It is not an accident that the most strongly individualistic and anti-bureaucratic groupings of modern America overlap largely the religious sects with the greatest expectancy of personal encounters with their god. (This, incidentally, may explain the "mystery" to many people of how the suave Hollywood product Ronald Reagan came to be allied with the simple direct primitive evangelical Christians; he was a "rugged individualist," anti-bureaucratic.)

The belief in gods arising from "faith" is a step away from personal encounters and authoritative testimonials. "Faith" is an affirmation. As such it is taboo in logic, for logic is grounded upon reasons and proofs. Logic would not exist if faith had its way. Faith cannot be proven, but it can never be driven from its deep psychological recesses; it can only be surrendered. What is reported by a triumphant rationalism as the "destruction" of faith must always remain the dubious word of a third party. If the believer resists the terms of surrender, faith will never be conquered.

Faith cannot prove itself by logic, but it can be justified by its effects. "See how happy is the person who believes. If you would be happy, believe!" If the faithful receive more than the usual share of what are regarded as the goods of life, their faith acquires a pragmatic proof, different from and inaccessible to empirical proof. Insofar as "the goods of life" are psychic and exoterrestrial, one can construct an infallible circle from which the non-faithful are excluded. One can come from heaven, live bathed in heavenly light, and return to heaven, invulnerable to mundane contradiction.

Let one step for a moment out of the charmed circle into competition for mundane "goods of life" and one finds oneself amidst a crowd of the variously successful where statistics come into play, and one can no longer be sure that faith is associated with achievement. "God must love the poor; he made so many of them," it is said. Moreover, if the "goods" are doubted and "faith" as a good is committed to definition, debate, and proof by conduct, then evil is the lot and behavior of many of the "real" faithful. "Faith moves mountains," says the Gospel of Mark (II: 22-4), but faith in whom, and to where are the mountains moved?

"Faith, hope, and charity," are supplicated by Paul the Apostle, but faith in its uttermost recess may be another word for the strong and unquenchable hope of a divine existence. Scientific psychologists will agree; faith is an attitude established by, preserved by, or destroyed by all that makes, maintains, and breaks other attitudes and predispositions: as for instance, drinking and smoking, quarreling, charitability, studiousness, political party affiliations, etc. All this is what concerns a college course in developmental psychology: the workings of indulgences and deprivations of infancy, family life, and society systematically and authoritatively explained. Faith is educed as a pattern of expectations, endorsed and rewarded, such that the faithful one, under normal conditions, will never regret his course of life nor lose his expectations.

Besieged and buffeted in its last traditional trenches by modern science, faith nevertheless survives, because nothing else survives better, because the desperate refugees from science and reason crowd in with it, and because a variety of non-traditional licenses are granted to privateers who venture to vest their faith in ancient astronauts, flying saucers, and the like.

Philosophical arguments for the existence of the divine can scarcely capture the popular imagination and suffuse popular religion with practical implications and a precise operative morality. A mention of the traditional arguments for the existence of god may illuminate the problem.

There is first the argument of the necessary reality of perfection: if we can conceive of the idea of a perfect being, the being must exist, because existence is an aspect of perfection. We join most philosophers in refusing this argument. A great deal of nonsense exists in the human mind, product of its inner machinations; must it all be granted the status of reality somewhere, sometime, someplace? All the monsters of fairy tales and science fiction would come alive. Dante's *Inferno* would be awaiting its newest victims even now.

Most conceivable things do not exist. Nor can we make them exist by an act of will, by the mechanism that has been called "omnipotence of thought," although we can make them exist as operative forces in people's minds, as illusions. Furthermore, we know that people lie in part according to their illusions, in all areas of existence - politics, love, economics, beauty, etc. Illusions have consequences. Hence if the consequences of a belief in a being of specific absolute perfection are good, or at least better than the consequences of any substitutable illusion, we may seek earnestly to establish and maintain the illusion, or myth (for that is what it is as well.)

A second traditional argument for the existence of god pleads that the world as we see it cannot have come about without a previously existing cause. Since the universe is so grand and so complex, containing by definition everything, its cause must be at least as great, conforming to what may be called god, the demiurge, the first cause, the creator. Everything does have a precedent form - call it a sense. This we sense; and every experiment can probably prove it.

But it may be of the nature of the world to extend itself indefinitely in an infinity of forms occupying time and space or a presently unimaginable dimension. Hence the gods as creators are unnecessary. One may slide into a counter-assertion to prove their existence: that the gods are in the principle of change, there being no ultimate reason for change other than the will of a demiurge, who may be Aristotle's "unmoved mover," or Heraclitus' inherent changefulness of all things. So close are such abstractions to scientific generalities, so far removed from practical religion, and so vulnerable to contradiction (for all things can be viewed in their unchanging aspects à la Parmenides), that the gods would soon shuffle off to Sheol with their help.

The most popular of arguments for the existence of gods is the (humanly perceived) design of the world. So marvelous are the construction and interconnections of things and so purposeful (that is, moving towards their proper goals) that an infinitely masterful designer must have created the universe. However, even before modern science exposed some of the guts of the material world, including the physiology of psychology, philosophers, priest, and ordinary people were acutely aware of the evils of the world. They were aware that the world had been nearly destroyed on occasion by natural (divine) forces, so that the gods came to represent destructiveness as well as constructiveness.

Under such conditions, the problem of evil was tied into the grand design, so that interminable arguments might occur concerning what parts of the world and its people were deliberately designed by the gods to malfunction. The tedium of this discussion hardly assists in any proof of divine design, while the issue keeps people in a prolonged and useless state of fear and quarrelsomeness.

To be sure, a great many processes of the world seem to be moving toward a definable end. Thus, the common astronomical theory is that the sun will ultimately burn itself out; so is the idea already cited that the present fragmented universe of starry bodies was created by a primordial explosion, but that a limit of expansion will be reached, whereupon the universe will implode. Again it is often said that man will colonize space, etc. All such processes appear to be non-random, hence to some thinkers, purposeful.

Take the biological "law" that evolution cannot reverse itself. If this is so, evolution appears to have some goal, which encourages certain theorists to feel better about the world and others to believe in gods. Materialists can take a different view: non-random processes develop an evermore specific direction out of inertia; once an ear begins to evolve in animals, it will develop into various ears unless it finally quantavolutes; the developing ear preempts some proportion of the changeability of the organism. Therefore, an "end" or "purpose" can be claimed. It is hardly an occasion for divine pride, or for pride in the divine. And sense organs may degenerate in evolution, not only among blind moles, but in man, whose senses are stunted by comparison with those of others species.

With an irresistible thrust, most theistic religions have promoted the idea that "nothing is impossible to the gods," The gods are usually allowed perfection. They are eternal, omnipotent, omniscient, omnipresent, omnivirtuous, unchanging and unchangeable (for how can perfection change?) So naive are such assignments of qualities, that they seem to be pure projected delusions. Just as one can solve a mathematical problem by manipulating the concept of infinity, one can arrange and interpret any divine action with the concept of complete qualities.

It seems that design is found where the heart is: one who is healthy, reared to optimism, indulged, and promoted in life, is likely to find better designs in what he senses and experiences than others find who are less blessed. Indeed, a goodly part of much religion consists precisely in designating the world as evil, in anticipation of our arriving shortly after death in a better world, or escaping presently from the world about.

The stress of religions upon suffering is unavoidable. Suffering is not only blatant in ordinary lives; it is also regurgitated as feelings out of history, not merely church and social history, but the history of great disasters engineered by the gods. Finally, suffering gestates in the very genetics of humanity, in its eternal fearfulness, in the contradiction between wishing for everything and controlling nothing.

At times, religious factions diverge and sects spring up which preach a religion of secular joy and the elimination of suffering and sorrowful memory. But secular joy as religion soon liquidates the religion. The joy of religion generally must consist in the appreciation of man's lot and a surcease from it upon death, or resurrection, or otiose earthliness.

The philosopher Immanuel Kant perceived in the moral laws always present among human beings a proof of the existence of god. Unlike the beasts, men rule themselves by voluntary ethics, it is said. This unique and universal search for the good suggests a divine purpose. Only the magnificent order of the heavens, which moved Kant to "ever-increasing wonder and awe," was comparable to "the moral law within me."

Modern quantavolution readily demonstrates the inconsistency of the order of heavens. As contrasted with older generations of scientists, the younger generation sees more and more the history of the heavens as of quantavolutions and catastrophes. Ethology and socio-biology meanwhile are asserting vigorously the presence, now here and now there, in animals and plants, of moral rules and moral behavior that man used to regard as products of his superior and voluntary ethics.

As for the "moral law of man," sociologist Louis Wirth used to remark to his students that "people differ in every way that they can." A thoroughly relativistic and pragmatic philosopher would add that it is "the moral law within me" which causes most of the worst human conflicts in this world. I agree with both men. The claim to know gods, so general in history and today, has not reduced differences so much as it has promoted fights over them.

CHAPTER FOUR

THE HEAVENLY HOST

The animation of nature is an instinctual interpretation, primordial with humankind. It occurs with humans today, more obviously among the young. To exorcize it takes training.

The earliest gods took shape as the Sky and Earth. There developed next a more definitely formed solar god of the Sky. A change in nature was responsible for the change in divine forms. Logically, and in accord with most evidence of what was manifest, the primordial welkin was densely packed, without brilliant separated lights, until the sky was broken up and these appeared. The great god would have come first in his solar (or planetary) form if the sky had been penetrable.

Until nearly 2700 years ago, the skies were periodically invested with changing forms, and much of this turbulence was impacting upon the Earth physically, as well as upon the minds of humans. The scene was conducive to polytheism. Divine presences of all types might be discerned. Yet there was usually a great god, a father of gods, an Ouranos, a Kronos or a Zeus.

We infer from this fact that such beings were at some time most impressive features of the sky and, when they were not, were scalding memories, which had so dominated the human setting that no successor, no matter how prominently active, could match what its "ancestor" or "father" had achieved.

Some cultures, such as the Roman, Greek, and Hindu, did not conceal the succession of fathers, and assigned family roles to junior actors, while the Hebrews over a period of time accepted the Mosaic rationalization which fitted several great gods into a unity. This did not come without ideological and political struggles of great intensity and long duration, some of which are recounted, in expurgated form, in the Old Testament.

"Varro had the diligence to collect thirty thousand names of gods - for the Greeks counted that many. These were related to as many needs of the physical, moral, economic, or civil life of the earliest times." He found 40 Hercules alone. So writes Giambattista Vico. The sacred book of the *Mahàbàrata* (1: 39) claims 33,333 Hindu deities, and later sources say that there were a thousand times as many. The Nordic *Grimnismal* gives over 50 names to Odin. The Babylonian *Emunia Elis* culminates in a recital of 50 names of Marduk. In the history of symbolism and language, words may actually have begun as god-names. Words might have been more sacred than pragmatic, until an advanced state of collective amnesia and sublimation had been achieved. Even today, a great many people cannot adapt to the idea that words are not real hard things.

If the Greeks had 30,000 god-names, and the Hindus even more, then all the world's cultures must have had hundreds of thousands. The great numbers, however, reduces to a comprehensible order when a proper theory is applied to them. The total of this heavenly host includes, first, a few great gods, whose real existence in the sky lent structure to the ages. Second, occur the thousands of names of the great gods, most of which have yet to be identified with their referents. Many of these names are concealed references; others are what foreign cultures call a certain culture's gods; some names isolate a quality of the gods; some names are used to marry the gods of one culture to those of another.

The principle of ambivalence (in the form of opposites) leads to the division of great gods into gods and devils. Here the human mind seeks to control the gods by projection of benevolence and beneficence upon a good god, and malevolence and maleficence upon a bad god or devil, hoping that the one will outwit and outstruggle the other. Devils have invariably extruded from an animated religious setting, there being no way of exorcizing them from man's primordially established soul. In the Hebraic complex, god cannot commit evil; if a bad effect is deemed evilly inspired, it is attributed to the devil.

Some religions have merged the contradiction of good and evil into the same god, who holds different names for his given qualities and exercises benevolent or malevolent impulses for inscrutable reasons, or for "obvious" reasons, or for reasons not to be inquired about. The Greek gods were rather of this type. One significant result of the differences may be in the potential intensity of the "guilt complex." The Greco-Roman pagans suffered less from guilt-feelings than their Christian counterparts. Such gods may acquire many appellations, some of them contradicting others. New appellations may also serve to avoid the designation of new gods, an ever-present "problem" in a polytheistic system.

Appellations may thus be congruent and complementary, that is, logical and harmonious qualities that a single personality may possess. Or they may appear nonconforming, leading non participating observers (enemies or scientists) to question the nature of the god. However, as with great contradictions - " God vs. Devil" - so with lesser contradictions - "god of arts vs. god of war" - the contradiction might be only apparent, the same supernatural being having apparently produced a variety of effects during his primary effective manifestations in nature. Thus Mercury-Hermes is both thief and healer. And Santillana and von Dechend refer to "the baffling Mesopotamian texts dealing with gods cutting off each other's necks and tearing out each other's eyes."

In the eternally agonizing search for a great god with whom one might co-exist peacefully, those who followed the path of opposites have been plagued by the possibly triumphant fearful powers of the devil, whereas those who pursued the path of the contradictions had to admit the mutability of their god and the impossibility of more than incessant recurrent reconciliations between god and people.

Another major source of divine names (besides the attributions) is the outcome of processes of memory and forgetting. To forget the disasters that characterized the appearance of the gods was urgently demanded by the bruised mind; but any lapse of memory would be accompanied by fear that god will not permit himself to be forgotten and will punish forgetfulness. The mind then works to define and characterize god so that his image will be tolerable upon the conscious level. It further adds new words to its vocabulary of the divine, discovering that a god called by another name is less threatening. Still further, by the logic of delusion, a god whose name is mysterious or hidden will respect the awe and fear bound up in the secrecy, and at the same time will restrict himself to activities that do not threaten the very core of terror that crouches in the human soul. A plethora of non-names, secret and cult-names, and common partial names comes forth.

Effects of many kinds are produced, the least of which is the confusion of names that confronts the outside observer; the selective remembering is tolerable; occult elites can dominate societies; the language and concepts of a people are enriched as the naming of gods flows through the symbolic world by association, analogy, and implication.

Although some thousands of names are those of great gods in one form or another, other thousands are assigned to angels, minor devils, minor divinities, spirits, divinized natural phenomena of the earth, air, water, fire, plants and animals, divine heroes, and divine kings. This myriad of names also possesses its logic. Prior to human creation the names could not exist: there was not stimulus, impulse, or mechanisms. Once the mind had exploded into self-awareness, however, a great many beings might move into it.

Limits to the number of names were set by the "behavior" of such beings, there being more sub-gods in disastrous than in peaceful times. The need for alleviation of anxiety occasions a sort of subconscious shifting of cargo with an invention and appeal to a new god following the failure of performance of an old one. The logical operation or reduction of "beings" is useful, when, for purposes of control, fewer sub-gods are needed. Finally, the ability of the inventor to achieve collective consensus may sometimes fail; no doubt heroic charisma or priestly office allows one to designate a new god only to a degree.

But, while these factors restrain the process, in any given culture the number of supernatural beings is apparently magnified by the telling of tales from foreign and destroyed cultures; these beings of course enter the mind only as subordinates or evil opposites of one's own gods. Moreover, as in classical Greek mythology, supernatural beings pile their traits and presence upon the true beings of the culture until, to the undiscerning mind, they become indistinguishable from the humans; the totality of divinities and spirits becomes a seemingly nonsensical mass.

By analogy with the cultures of modern tribes, and by reference to surviving cave drawings and artifacts, it would seem that people are naturally inclined to perceive gods in all aspects of nature. This perception is true insofar as the gods of creation must be assumed to be genetically behind every divine or spiritual (supernatural) communication, symbol, and image. It is also natural even among apes (The neuter gender, the "it," is itself probably a product of divinely inspired categorization; "it" is needed not for inanimate objects, as school children are told, but for a godly presence that is neither female nor male.)

The collective experience and interpersonal communication of an event that requires a naming - an event whose connection with the numerous high-energy expressions of nature is obvious, but whose direct efficient cause is not a great god - is a final way by which many a demigod is produced.

Thus the breezes are named, the meteors, the volcanoes, the erratic boulders, the deeps of caves and seas, the ancient trees, the animals of curious form and expression, and so on to many thousands. Then, too, the early kings, the kings of crises, their mothers, the sorcerers, saints, inventors, prophets, and so on to many more thousands of the divine and semi-divine. Then, further, the products of their work: "devil's hole," "angel rock," "Mount Zeus," "Meteora," and so on through a world whose geography - that was once worked upon by the gods - belatedly and usually mistakenly accredits the heavenly host via a largely invented name. All of these processes of naming are consistent with and dependent upon the primordial appearances of the gods.

The saints of several Christian churches are a form of minor divinity, who are deemed to have performed celestial miracles, given great social services, communed with the Lord, or served gloriously in battle. Saint Joan of Arc comes readily to mind. Periods of natural and social crisis are their favored setting. The Hindus, who do not draw scholastic distinctions so fine, have created divinities of the same order. Thus the villages of West Bengal worship Sitala, Goddess of smallpox, though smallpox no longer troubles the area. R. W. Nicolas has found the origins of Sitala in the 18th century, upon an unprecedented outburst of the plague. Bengali doctors soon became preeminent in their analysis and treatment of smallpox, using variolation. Simultaneously, the disease was ascribed to Sitala, who had been born late among the gods and found none who knew how to worship her. So she chose to infect especially children with the pox, for "a late-coming goddess required such terrible weapons." Hers became an annual and major rite, accompanied by processions, animal sacrifices, and music. When the plague was absent, she was also served, for "both the presence and absence of disease are manifestations of the grace of the Mother." One notes the psychic need, that science cannot fill, to displace blame to a divine party, to turn punishment by the God back upon the self, and to propitiate and thank the divinity for not exerting its full powers if bestowing evil.

Divinity has often been assigned to kings and emperors. Egyptian, Assyrian, Roman, Chinese, Japanese, and the rulers of other cultures were considered gods, and worshiped in life and death. They have been pronounced by themselves and their associated elites as a relatives of gods or even one of the gods. This practice, so repulsive to democrats, is a means by which an elite and the people it rules can deal with and control the gods. At the same time, rule by divine kings is easier, because the source of the rule is a god. His claim to divinity varies with the secularism of the elite and masses, so that it is by no means rare that the god is usurped, overthrown, and killed.

In some forms of society, now extinct, kings were not only gods or semi-divine, but were used as sacrifices regularly or in emergencies (often but by no means always in the form of temporarily appointed surrogates).

We see once again, as we do repeatedly and more clearly than in other life spheres, the basic functioning of religion to secure humans from fear of celestial disasters, and all fears of matters deemed to be connected with the heavens gone astray and chaotic. The Japanese Emperor used to be regarded as a god and was compelled to severely restrain his movements upon critical occasions, such as during some unusual celestial phenomenon. This catatonic state was believed to restrain the gods and heavens; if the god emperor does not change even his countenance, one believed, the countenance of heaven will not change either.

The puzzle of the god-heroes, with their half-and-half ancestry, still occupies us. Why must there be everywhere these hundreds of men and women who muddy the waters of great gods?

Typical explanations are unsatisfactory. It is said that gods and god-heroes are the same - a truth, but too limited a truth to answer the question. Others say that people want to be descended from gods, as, later, we shall see that they cannibalize their gods. This also is apparent. And some are content to say that gods are really only big heroes. Because of such explanations and simply because of the inordinate confusion from the plethora of names and deeds, the truth behind myth is difficult to find and, indeed, few are ready to believe there is a truth.

A quantavolutionary explanation of who and what are god-heroes can be set forth for what it's worth. God-heroes are sublimatory. When, in periods following the direct and evident appearance and behavior of natural gods, there occurs a lull and a stability, humans, continuing their search of means to control the gods, begin the process of denying their existence by humanizing them. If people were left to pursue this process, the gods would be ultimately erased from the human mind (and history). The first phase, that is, consists of direct experience of gods in nature. The second phase permits god-heroes, the third phase pure heroes, and the fourth phase calls for plain human beings with typical human behaviors. To take an example: Mars is Ares; Ares becomes Hercules; Hercules is a god, but also Hercules becomes human, first as a god-hero; Hercules becomes quite human; Hercules becomes subject of a mass of folk tales; the unconscious artistic mind can push to all limits of the imagination with him.

What halts the process of losing gods entirely? On occasion (and many live in such expectations), the gods reappear, wreak havoc, and, so, self-sufficient, unassisted, full and direct god ship is restored. At the same time, the most obsessive and schizoid officials and prophets outlast the social sublimation that is occurring, and insist that gods *directly* are the only *authorities,* and will not let the process of creating god-heroes go too far.

Then, too, a minor phenomenon occurs, which is incorrectly elevated to the major explanation by uniformitarianism and psychic monolithics: pride of ancestry; elite self-elevation, etc.; "credenda et miranda" of ruling groups. Heroes are built into a group's history: "A treason it is to deny them." "We can't eliminate god-heroes without denying the gods." That is, the heroes of a ruling class are made divine. This, we stress, does happen but is not the primary and independent cause of gods and god-heroes. The gods impregnated themselves in the god-heroes.

There is little question that Campbell has succeeded in telling the universal plot of the hero found throughout the world from the most ancient times.

"The standard path of the mythological adventure of the hero is a magnification of the formula represented in the rites of passage: separation - initiation - return....

A hero ventures forth from the world of the common day into a region of supernatural wonder: fabulous forces are there encountered and a decisive victory is won: the hero comes back from this mysterious adventure with the power to bestow boons on his fellow men."

How does this universal and even obsessive plot of mankind relate to the theory of quantavolution? Simply, we think. First we note the cycle: the going forth ends in the return. Second, the world of the hero begins ordinarily, though almost always with premonitions and prophecy; indeed the ordinary may be actual nothingness. This may be interpreted as a regular order of the universe. Next come the disastrous experiences: a succession of personalized natural forces beat against the hero, testing his will to survive, and to control himself and the human and natural environment. When the forces have subsided or have been defeated, the hero returns to a stable social order upon which he bestows his moral and material gains.

The career of the hero thus mirrors the career of the gods, who mirror the career of nature. At first, the tie to gods is direct; imitation is permissible, but not "heroic myth," which would be considered intolerable insolence by the gods. Only after a period of the suppression of experiences, and after a working out of psychic methods of dealing with them, can a human act out the plot of the gods and be called god-names. Once the process is begun, however, it has no end of sublimated ramifications until the gods are treated cavalierly and even desacralized - until the next catastrophic event.

Campbell joins himself to the psychoanalytic school that regards gods as non-existent psychological means for the human to jump beyond the ordinary world into the imaginary world; "gods are only convenient means to the ineffable." They, and myth, help the mind to transcend phenomena and achieve the great void or openness of spirit. Although this theory is functionally true, it is very limited, and without realization of the grave primordial dependence of the human mind upon the real events of its history and of nature.

Connections between divinities or sacred things and stars are usually the result, not of the activity of the stars nor of the playful resort to placing fairy tales among the stars, but of the fixing of the location from which a great event appeared to originate. The Deluge of Noah, by its many designations, is connected in widely-separate countries with the planet Saturn, but also with the star-cluster known as the Pleiades; some grave event affected the sky and earth when the Pleiades could somehow represent effects of Saturn. Scorpio is the background setting from which cometary Venus launched herself on a destructive swoop upon Earth. Scorpio is identified, if not before the event, then after the event, in new associations with the event. Early and later events occur in connection with Scorpio and by extension are associated with the Venus episode. Myths of one time and character become mixed up with others later on. The stars themselves, alone or in clusters, come to acquire legendary histories, and, as such, acquire future functions as places of resort or transubstantiation or limbo for worldly or otherworldly heroes, people, and divinities.

Plato insisted that the stars "are not small, as they appear to the eye, but each of them is immense in bulk." Further, every solid body of heaven had "a soul attached" to it. Thus Proclus, in his commentary on Plato's *Timaeus,* declares that each celestial god has angels, demons, and heroes who are phases and extensions of it. And usually these characters have abodes or posting places in the sky. The rich Polynesian legends carry their heroes on many travels that are often imagined as terrestrial and maritime but which originated as travels of gods though the vast stellar and planetary regions. In one of its dimensions, the legend of the Argonauts is of a sky voyage that carried the adventurers to Circe (Corsyra, the Boreal Circle) where the island of Drepane ("sickle") lay, beneath which was buried the sickle of Kronos.

Much of what might be told of angels is sung by Rainer Maria Rilke. Here we have the multi-faceted visions, the mixed love and terror, the mirroring of the human mind, and the sense of co-creatures of genesis long ago.

> *Every angel is terrible. Still, woe to me,*
> *I sing to you, near fatal birds of the soul,*
> *full-knowing of you...*
> *Early-achieved and over-indulged of creation,*
> *you high ridges, dawn-reddened peaks of all genesis,*
> *- pollen of the flowering godhead,*
> *links of light, halls, steps, thrones,*
> *welkins, shields of joy, uproars of stormy ecstasies —*
> *beauty then suddenly, singly*

mirrors scooping up outpoured beauty
back into your own faces.

To the quantavolutionist, the presence of naturally occurring "angels" is logical and historical. More puzzling is whether they were comets, planets, or meteorites. Thus, the astronomers Strube and Napier attempted a natural history of the encounters between Earth and comets, and argue that in the early days of mankind disastrous comets were variously named and, when they had retired to the farther reaches of the solar system, or had crashed, or broken up, their natures and behaviors were assigned to the planets who were the regularly eccentric movers of the solar system.

That is, they would deny the asseverations of those such as Santillana, von Dechend, Velikovsky, Milton and myself who assigned the active roles in legends to the planets, and, in the case of the last three, give large changes in motion and behavior to all of the planets such as to fulfill the requirements of some angelic behaviors. This is not to say that comets did not occur, but that their original creation and impetus arose out of planetary explosions and disturbances. Too, it may be borne in mind that any body changing its movement in space will behave as a comet, growing horns and tails and trails and presenting a variety of apparitions.

It will take many years of study, and even then it may be impossible, to determine the historicity of the celestial solid body identity of even the more important "angels" and "sky-heroes" of world legend. Dwardu Cardona, in his studies of the Archangel Michael and others, has set an example of what must be done on a large scale to eliminate the confusion of planets and angels.

Humans have been polytheistic even when their ruling religion states that one god and only one god exists. The people (and usually, too, their religious guides) establish a heavenly host (including devils) to complement, supplement, and assist the supreme god. So it was in the beginning and ever thereafter.

The propaganda for monotheism is massive, so that people claim to believe in one god while worshiping many. The monotheistic illusion occurs in two forms. First, monotheistic affirmations are made by people who upon psychological investigation obviously mean different things by the word "god." Thus, a sample of the American people in 1982 indicates that all except 2% believe in god.

If the same people were interviewed in greater depth, however, different 'gods' would emerge: a punitive god, a loving god, a *deus otiosus*, a god who pries into every nook and cranny of every mind, a helping god, a god who helps those who help themselves, a very human 'old man', an abstract principle of good, a god of true believers, a god of all people, and so on. Some people feel close to god, others not. God confides in some humans, but such an idea seems preposterous to other believers.

Then, other divinities would appear: the Holy Trinity, Christ the Son, the Virgin Mary, the Holy Ghost, each taking some godlike qualities upon themselves, supremely competent in some regard. Saints, agents of god, would appear in abundance. Many person's religious mentation and practices are given over to a saint, whose direct protection and assistance one feels to be superior to those services obtained from god the Father or God the Son; these latter, it seems, "are never there when you need them." The devil comes up with some or many divine qualities, almost always evil but "doing god's work," and god is often deemed helpless, even if by his own will, to rid the world of the devil.

Historical and contemporary heroes, such as George Washington and the incumbent President, find themselves contending with saints for the possession of divine qualities and the performance of miracles. In sum, a great variety of gods exists in fact under the name of The God. Such people may still be called monotheistic, so long as we understand the limits of this term.

Then, other peoples of the world confess to more than one god. Such are the Hindus and Taoists, for instance. They need not agree, either, on the definition of the gods of their pantheon, any more than the Teutons, Greeks, or Romans would have agreed upon theirs. A peculiarity of the Hebrew religion of Moses was its very early achievement of an abstraction of the Lord which permitted an easier succession of gods (so long as integrity of a Hebrew nation was preserved). This is so despite many deviations and polytheistic cults, and much editing of the story to stress the unity of the Lord.

Not all early Hebrews were devout worshiper of Yahweh alone. Also, several rebellions against Moses were directed at his special, all-inclusive, exclusive god, Yahweh. Theologians have occasionally surmised, and correctly, I think, that Aaron, High Priest of the Jews under Moses, would have been fully tolerant of the worship of Baal, and that by Baal was indicated possibly more than one god besides

Yahweh, possibly Saturn, Mercury, and Venus (to employ planetary representatives who had many parochial names.)

When Korah and his followers rebelled against Moses, one of their principal complaints, which has not been fully excised from the Bible and is also the subject of legend, was his suppression of their freedom to commune directly with the Lord. One encounters the same demand among the English Levellers of the Seventeenth Century, now raised against Oliver Cromwell, their Mosaic leader of the protestant revolution against the Crown. One god, the rebels are told, means a monotheism both of god and worshiper, by authoritative definition. This other kind of anarchistic monotheism cannot be tolerated by a theocratic regime. Else every person would have his own god.

Jewish legends, which should be generously interpreted in the face of the monotheistic propaganda, accord a place for religious beliefs and practice connected with the Holy Spirit, the Archangels Michael and Gabriel (both identified with planets), the Moon, hosts of angels, characters out of Sheol, and the Devil. Legends speak of these entities cordially and understandingly, as well as accusingly. From these stories and the historical record, it is clear that the victory of Yahweh was never complete among the Jews, and that much of the time he was "the professional man's god," the god of priests, military officers, and most kings and judges.

And so it went thereafter; the seekers and executors of "the Truth" sponsored monotheism. Moses was a scientist as well as a monotheist, I have concluded from my study of his life. Akhnaton, monotheist Pharaoh of the Eighteenth Dynasty of Egypt, proclaimed his slogan as Truth *ma'at,* and was overthrown by polytheistic priests and populace. I suspect that he derived his monotheism from the Levant where he spent his childhood, perhaps even from Israel.

Polytheistic societies have had their monotheists, often connected with a free-thinking intelligentsia, akin to scientists. Thus, around 500 B. C., we find the Greek Xenophanes saying, "There is one god" (Fragment 23), and "He sees as a whole, thinks as a whole, and hears as a whole" (fragment 24). The philosophical discovery of a single god often, too, verges upon pantheism; the idea that "all things are full of gods" is not far from the idea that "god is in all things."

When the Romans put down the Jewish rebellions of the first century and ultimately dispersed the population, they acted partly in order to defend the principle of extending religious rights to all gods that would tolerate other gods. This the Yahwists would not accept.

Meanwhile, the Christians, having promoted the Son of Man to become the Son of God, and then to become an identity united to a redesigned Yahweh, penetrated the larger population of the Roman Empire. They were persecuted as often as not on grounds that they would not tolerate other gods, or worship the divine aspects of the secular power latent in monotheism; nor could the regimes succeeding to the Empire integrate the Christian doctrine firmly into their moral and legal order. The Byzantine Empire accomplished the first unification. Only after a thousand years from its legitimization, could certain western regimes quite dominate monotheism.

For this triumph, they required a weakened Roman Catholic Church, a theory of divine right of monarchs, and ultimately popular nationalism that in democratic form placed god and country in the hands of the "people." There came then in government and industry the theory of centralization, carefully developed over centuries by the church and embodied in many ideas, ranking from that of papal infallibility to proofs of the existence of god built upon absolute and extreme values.

Finally, monotheism could obtain support from science because science derived support from monotheism. Science has been a greater exponent and defender of monotheism than has traditional Christianity. Almost all scientists who have confessed to a religious belief have been deists, that is, believers in a god whose qualities and behavior bordered upon the laws of Nature. Nature (" herself," we note in a singular transposition of sex) tends to acquire among scientific religious believers and scientific non-believers much of the omniscience, purposefulness, immanence, transcendence, power, absoluteness, lawfulness, orderliness, and responsiveness to human goodness and sin otherwise characteristic of the single deity. There is widely believed to be only one truth, one *ma'at*, in science.

In addition, then, to its other peculiar historical features, mosaic monotheism operates still as a vital feature in the ideological, hence structural, processes of modern religions of the Hebraic complex, in conventional bureaucratic and single-headed (especially charismatic) governments, in judicial fictions (such as "finding the law"), in international politics, in science, in pedagogy, in communist (but hardly "Marxist") regimes, in traditional philosophy as in most humanistic disciplines, and, of course, in the family.

The sociological treatise whose writing we are imagining would probably conclude that some of the most powerful and pervasive influences of monotheism have been manifested in "enlightened" secularized processes of the scientific revolution of the 17th to 19th centuries, and the largely secular political history of the 18th to 20th centuries. Nothing of this should surprise us. Religion, we have already explained, seeps into all things.

A final comment on the effects of monotheism may be in order. Elsewhere, in *Homo Schizo I and II,* I explained the grave and genetic human problem of combining the several egos naturally emanating from the structure of the human mind into a single ego, "a person who can live with himself." A percipient authority once termed the ancient Greeks schizophrenic, and central in the syndrome of their behavior was their polytheism. We can surmise that monotheism was not available to them to help "get their heads together."

Further, we say that monotheism fashions a therapy for one kind of schizophrenia by creating another kind. It allows an orderly mind by pushing every object and tension onto one or the other pole - oneself or a god. In line with what we have already said of the effects and function of monotheism in society and science, we can expect from the monotheistic homo schizo a more orderly and consistent accretion of symbols and a greater psychological penchant for mental discipline and linear logical forms (as opposed to artistic, analogical and intuitive modes of thought). Monotheism thus can serve as a tool of inquiry in seeking to understand why certain groups and individuals historically and today have more disciplined minds, are logically consistent, and are superior at scientific investigation and human organization. We stress once more, however, that monotheism does not clearly distinguish religions - all being polytheistic in one or more senses - but that a belief that one is monotheistic may create special qualities in oneself

CHAPTER FIVE

LEGENDS AND SCRIPTURE

The biggest difference between myth or legends and sacred scriptures is that the latter are selected legends, called "divinely inspired or spoken" by their believers, which have been carefully guarded and edited to pursue the continuous but also continually changing religious goals of their custodians. Myth and legends, not so regarded, or whose line of custodians died out, were left like abandoned children to wander through time as casual history and unconstrained imagination, until caught up by scientific mythological studies.

Giambattista Vico was the first modern scholar to perceive this process when, two centuries ago, he wrote:

> The fables in their origins were true and severe narrations, whence mythos, fable, was defined as *vera narratio* (a true account)... But because they were originally for the most part gross, they gradually lost their original meanings, were then altered, subsequently became improbable, after that obscure, then scandalous, and finally incredible. . . These are the seven sources of the difficulties of the fables...

One of many debts that we owe to Plato is his respect for myth and legend. He, too, fulminated at those who dismissed or, worse, corrupted history by their misuse of legends. In my sceptically minded exploration of the story of the destruction of Atlantis, the attitude of Plato mitigated my doubts. Plato goes out of his way to insist that the story be taken seriously, despite its prehistoric origins. Critias, his protagonist, is given to claim repeatedly that he heard and learned the story from his grandfather as a true and exact account.

Significantly, to a modern mnemologist, Critias declared that although he had forgotten much of what he had heard of the previous day's discussions, he had forgotten none of what he had learned as a child about Atlantis.

The Atlantis story is generally disbelieved, yet if an educated unbeliever were to compare it with the story of the Deluge of Noah in the Bible, it would appear to be just as (im)plausible. It is no less specific. The "author" of one is Plato, of the other, Moses; who is more reliable? True, Atlantis is no longer to be found, above or below the sea, and therefore presumed not to have sunk; but the flood that climbed to great heights all over the Near East has vanished, too. Objectively, one would have to be as sceptical (and no more so) about the one account as about the other. The difference is that a great many millions of people believe in the Noachian Deluge because they believe in its sacred format, while the Atlanteans are long dead and the moral of their story - that Zeus destroyed them because he found their squabbling and vices intolerable - no longer lives in people's minds.

A legend is history which has been largely unconstrained by realism and objectivity since the happenings that it describes. The boundary zone between legend and history is, of course, thickly populated. Thus, we have the well-known legend of the founding of Rome by close descendants of Aeneas, exiled prince of Troy, who settled in Latium. Many ancient scholars believed the story. Most Romans accepted it as true. The actual beginnings of the legend occur before Virgil, who related it in his epic poetry. If historical, the legend should go back to the also legendary beginnings of Rome, in the Eighth Century B. C. Then it was that Romulus and Remus, grandsons of Aeneas, built the town.

But while scholars have accepted the legend's time of the founding, the Eighth Century, they have rejected the Aeneas story because the last war of Troy was placed in the Twelfth Century or earlier. However, recent studies have emptied Greek chronology of four to five centuries of time, which would permit placing Aeneas within a century of Romulus and Remus. To confirm the connection is a task of future research, but in support of it is the important fact that when faced with a collection of practically all the evidence of art, archaeology, inscriptions, stories and ancient comment about the earlier times of Rome, one finds a striking gap in the collection extending between the 13th and 8th centuries, as was manifested in the great Bimillennial Exposition of Virgiliana held at Rome in 1982.

Another case of the interplay among history, legend, and scripture may be offered. It concerns the Christian Gospels of the life and work of Jesus. These are four in number, all written some years after the death of Jesus, under circumstances that have never been clear. Furthermore, as the reader will acknowledge, attitudes towards the Gospels and Jesus have ranged from the denial that he ever existed, passing through an acceptance of the Gospels as generally or exactly true, to other extreme ideas such as that Jesus was a Jewish radical rebelling against Roman rule, whose story was censored in the Gospels.

Dr. Livio C. Stecchini, both an ancient historian and a historian of science, for several years before his death taught a college course on the trial of Jesus. There he developed a theory that Seneca, the Stoic philosopher, dramatist, and Roman statesman, was the basic source for the Gospels. His brother met Saint Paul of Tarsus when Paul was imprisoned in Rome awaiting trial and execution, and Seneca himself could have interrogated Paul at will, given his high state position. That the Stoic and Christian positions on many ethical issues were similar - more so than the Mosaic-Christian position - has been often remarked upon. That Jesus follows the birth history of many Greco-Roman heroes is manifest: His father being divine, his mother human.

Seneca, said Stecchini, composed a great tragedy, later lost, and upon its manuscript and/ or performances the Gospels drew very heavily. Thus it happened, as Stecchini has elaborated, that the plot of the trial and execution, the actions of the characters, and the timing and scenes of the Gospels are framed in the traditional structure of Greco-Roman drama.

As important as Stecchini's theory may be, we cannot treat it here as more than a conjecture. The conjecture, however, allows us to make a point about legend and scripture. To the studious non-believer, sacred scripture is forever the source of historiography and the analysis of myth and legend. Scripture may be dissected from as many perspectives and in as many ways as the creative and scientific mind can imagine and instrument. On the other hand, to the studious believer, sacred scripture is first of all literally true, and all that the creative mind can imagine must be consistent with the literal truth. Even if, by every empirical test that is respected by historical and natural science, Jesus were deemed to have never existed (an unlikely prospect), the believer can continue to believe in the holiness of his mundane being and therefore in the literalness of the gospels, just as the Roman Catholic believer asserts in the transubstantiation of bread and wine into the veritable body and blood of Christ in the Holy Communion.

What we should then, by scientific standards, possess would be an entirely fictional and mythical complex contained in identical form in millions of cerebro-neural systems governing a host of behaviors. The reality of these systems and behaviors cannot and would not be disputed by science. Science would say, here we have a purely delusional system to accompany the larger delusional system that is a mixture of history, legend, myth, and non-reality known as the Old Testament or Mosaic system. And if all of the Old Testament were empirically disproved (also very unlikely), the scientist would then retire to the same position, namely treating the total New Testament - Old Testament complex as a purely delusional system with behavioral consequences.

Myth may be defined as a religious and aesthetic interpretation, or story based upon legend and history. Its goal is to serve essentially non-historic functions while reminding its audience of a significant historical happening. Myth is closely related to rituals and sacrifices, which have the same goal, but, like sacred scriptures, are under severe theocratic constraints.

Myth is often indistinguishable from legend, but this occurs in part because the original culture to which a myth and legend belonged no longer exists to explain to us the difference between the two; myths and legends intermingle in a flow through time which we experience much later and find indistinctly composed of both. The famous myth of Phaeton, who drives the Sun's chariot, burns up the Earth, and is destroyed by a thunderbolt of Zeus, is by common standards today an entertaining myth, but appears upon investigation more and more as a legend supporting an historical intrusion of a cometary body upon the Earth's atmosphere.

Sacred scripture consists of authoritative prescriptions of various compounds of legend and myth, frequently describing rites and commands for their recital, together with moral judgments. All legends and myths of the most ancient kind contain some sacred quality, but scriptures enhance sacrality by ascribing their own origin to divine or divinely authorized sources.

Debating sacred scriptures is deemed to be arguing with god, which is not only useless but sacrilegious as well. One effect of this view is to allow only such discussions and research whose intended effects are to prove the scriptures correct in morals, rites, and history.

This situation is antithetic to scientific method, which permits only hypotheses, never absolute and eternal truth. Nevertheless it often happens that believers in holy scriptures, when justifying and proving them, cast many bones from their campfires into the darkness where the jackals of science prowl. The very insistence of literal Biblicists has driven scholars to test the authenticity of some reported events, thereupon to learn to their surprise that these can in fact be confirmed.

One of these was the dropping of manna among the hungry Israelites in the desert. Fitting precisely the details provided in the Bible and legendary sources to the conditions under which manna-like confections could be manufactured - electrical discharges, high temperatures, strange atmospheric gases, molecular compounding, etc. - a considerable degree of confirmation can be accorded to the Biblical story, enough to swing the scientific balance in its direction.

Once more, however, I would stress that by proving the capability of natural causes to have produced the Biblical "miracle," ordinary science erodes sacred scripture. It removes Yahweh from the manufacturing process and the product, and tends to make him a deistic god, that is, an ultimate cause or designer of manufacturing machinery.

Here, to be sure, Yahweh is still very close to events, according to Moses. But we recall that Moses is under suspicion of hallucinating; that is; another science, psychology, is working to erode the sacredness of the scripture, even while providing another form of natural explanation which authenticates in its own way the actions and speech conveyed in the scripture.

Sacred scriptures will always contain a high proportion of vague, indecipherable, incomprehensible, contradictory, and substantially untestable material. They will also have lost much, as historiographic methodology increasingly shows, owing to the alteration and accidents of their form of transmission, through cultural miscegenation, by reconciliation of older history with later history, by imposition of patterns of integration and new styles, by the collective amnesia that seeks both to forget actually and recall symbolically the traumas provoked in terrible ancient catastrophes, and by other changes in referents to accommodate ancient to present conditions, as a comet becoming a star, or as invisible electrical discharges which are now referred to as purely symbolic manifestations. Therefore there are limits to the scientificity that can be granted to the *Rig Vedas, Bible, Eddas, Book of the Dead, I Ching, Popul Vuh,* and other scriptures.

Nor can it benefit the credibility and influence of believers in sacred scriptures to be relegated by general consent, including their own, to the nonsensical remnants of the works. For example, many Biblical scholars refuse to employ or give credence to Talmudic commentaries and ancient legends of the Jews, when these documents will often testify to the authenticity of Biblical statements and elaborate them in a way that enhances their credibility.

Ominous conclusions emerge from these several pages. There is much history in myth, legend and scripture everywhere in the world. In a sense, all religions are desperately honest in their fundamental statements. Yet it is appreciated that, in a memory choice between a delusion and an historical fact, a religion will prefer the delusion. An attempt to "clean up" an historical religion by eliminating historical and empirical errors cannot succeed. Meanwhile we affirm that a religion cannot subsist on delusions alone: it must make historical and empirical statements. Are we to believe then that historical religion must be abandoned? We are not yet ready to answer this question.

CHAPTER SIX

RITUAL AND SACRIFICE

The Spanish conquistadors were appalled when they came upon extensive human sacrifices and cannibalism in Aztec Mexico some five centuries ago, and they killed an unnecessarily large number of this "master race" in the name of Jesus Christ. The bones were thrown to the dogs, which the Aztecs also liked to eat. An estimated two hundred and fifty thousand people were being killed and eaten annually, about one percent of the population of the whole region. It is argued by a student of the subject, Michael Harner, that this increment of meat went far toward making up for a serious protein deficiency in the Aztec diet.

When asked the reason for the sacrifices, which were conducted always with religious rituals, the Aztec spokesmen replied that the god managing the Sun depended on them. If the sacrifices were suspended, the Sun would not rise and set, and this glorious Age of the Sun would terminate in chaos. So quite aside from the matter of dietary protein, the stability of the cosmos was at stake. There had to be here, as elsewhere, a religious justification for cannibalism and human sacrifice.

The Spaniards were not impressed by this argument. They by now had many centuries of experience in confining their sacred cannibalism to the body and blood of Christ, which they absorbed whenever they partook of Holy Communion, which, if they were devout, ought to have been daily. The authority for this was Jesus Christ himself, as confirmed by no less than Saint Paul. This ritual sacrifice and cannibalism sufficed, and does to this day among the majority of Christendom. Nor did the Spaniards sacrifice animals, or even slaughter them ritually, which the ancient Jews, who almost always avoided any semblance of human sacrifice, faithfully performed according to the precepts of the Old Testament, and the Muslim followed suit.

No culture has been free of cannibalism in its history, nor are most religions that profess gods fully exempted today. Apparently cannibalism touches upon some vital nerve center of historical religion. Else there would be only the onetime universal practice, which would have been stopped, and there would not have continued the substituted sacrifice and eating of animals, nor the complicated symbolic sublimations whereby at the same moment religious believers both eat and do not eat human flesh. There has never been anything but sacred cannibalism except in dire life emergencies, such as occur now and then.

Actually it is easier to understand why cannibalism originated and flourished than why it has been severely constrained and, in some god-supporting religions, abandoned. Cannibalism, like killing others of his kind, is spontaneously human. It is a product of the set of mechanisms that generate when the self-aware, self-fearing human first appears. Seeing his alter ego in himself, he sees himself in other. He is continuously seeking to assimilate himself; he seeks to assimilate himself in others.

The identification with others is but a prelude to empowering himself by his ingestion of others. One does the same with the gods, here abetted in one's actions by the perceived behavior of the gods. The gods are frequently cannibalistic, he thinks. Gods fall to Earth or are cast down to Earth and are devoured. Gods encounter one another electrically in meteoritic and cometary forms in the sky, are split up, are attracted and repelled.

When Giorgio di Santillana comments on the "baffling" bloody battles of the gods in Mesopotamian legends, he might as well have spoken of all legend and of the cannibalism of the gods. It may always be moot whether men got their ideas of warfare, sacrifice, and cannibalism from the gods. They say so in holy writings, but who can trust sacred scripture and get a degree in astronomy without being as contradictory as the gods themselves?

A decline in celestial divine struggles, and in the horrendous fears incited thereby in humans, may explain why cannibalism has declined. The less fearful the human, the less inclined to sacrifice and the lesser the oblation. Man, it may be said to his credit, drives a hard bargain with his gods. The Aztec-Nahua rites were the last large-scale frank cannibalistic exercises, although small populations in Africa and Oceania pursued such practices until this century, and, from time to time, cannibalism is reported in chaotic and deprived human settings, as in Germany during the Thirty Years' war of the 16th century, and in Cambodia during the terrible Indochinese wars of the mid-twentieth century.

Yet the Aztecs were two thousand years removed from what we suggested were prime catastrophic motivators of cannibalism. So far as we know, the latest universal catastrophes brought on by exoterrestrial forces were in the eighth and seventh centuries before Christ. Later, however, Mexico and Central America were subjected to extremely heavy volcanism (related, we think, to the earlier exoterrestrial episodes) with clouds of ashes that darkened the days and obscured the sun.

None can scientifically estimate the duration of memories. Many of today's customs go back thousands of years, indeed probably to the very first men, so obdurate and obsessive is the transmission of collective experience. With occasional heavy disasters and appropriate mythology, a people can behave in the ways of their remote ancestors.

None can deny that some of the Israelis of today see themselves as reenacting the scenes of the Israeli conquest of Palestine of 3400 years ago. Prime Minister Begin was himself a "Moses buff" who enjoyed greatly long discussions about "those days" with other members of the "Club." Yet he appeared to all the world as a substantially secular figure, operating efficiently amidst high Twentieth Century technology.

Although anti-religious in a conventional sense, but professing a racial credo claimed to be consistent with ancient Teutonic legend, the Nazis of Germany between 1942-5 consigned millions of European Jews of all shades of religious belief to death by methodical gassing and burning. They murdered many millions of other Europeans, too. The routine, almost automatic procedures used for most of this holocaust, and the absence of traditional religious rituals in its execution, seem to remove it from the scope of religious study. No conventional religion would tolerate such conduct.

Still, the initial impulse, in Hitler and other Nazis, was that of "purification of the race" and the creation of a new master race (" chosen people") to rule the world. Nor did Hitler's status rank below that of the divine heroes of legend; his book, *Mein Kampf,* was given to newly-wed couples in place of the *Bible.*

The rituals frequently staged by the Nazi rulers of Germany were as spectacular and soul-stirring as any in history. The holocaust, however, was not a matter of public spectacle and in this regard was a source of sacrificial strengthening in the minds of some thousands who directly participated in the killings.

One might venture that these were special ceremonies reserved for the Nazi priesthood. There is small chance that the Nazi genocides would have stopped with the Jews. Gypsies were already suffering the same fate. The treatment meted out to civil populations in Eastern Europe teetered on the brink of genocide. If the Nazis had won World war II, there would have been ample opportunity to extend the holocaust in East Europe, Asia and Africa; a successful cleansing genocide of six millions might readily extend to sixty million, or until some historical accident would happen to stop the process.

Sacrifice and anthropophagy are still in the religions of a billion people and in the everyday life of almost totally secularized billions. The typical American follows the secular rules of eating, being very early in life told, "Don't just shove the food into your mouth." We are advised that "it is bad to eat between meals," we are told to "wash before coming to the table," to "set the table properly," to dress decently for dinner, eat the proper foods in the proper order, to serve foods in the proper order (' no dessert before the meat'), that father carves the meat, to leave a bit on the plate, to observe decorum at the table, and, in lesser numbers, to pray before every meal."

There are a hundred or more such typical rules of etiquette, rationalized as prophylaxis, "consideration for the feelings of others," and other particular explanations involving breeding and health. But there also were and are rules, of course, for the genteel cannibal, and well-educated sacrificer. The proverbial Englishman who used to dress for solitary dinner in the jungle was doing his part to hold the universe (and his own mind) intact. It was, of course, a joke when Cathedral Dean Jonathan Swift, viewing Ireland's dismal economic state in 1792, sardonically recommended that the poor sell their babies to the rich for eating.

Slater, a careful scholar of the Greek mind, thought the Greeks more mad than other peoples. Especially did they dwell in their myth upon parents eating their children. This he blamed upon the fathers for putting down the mothers, who thus, in fancy at least, revenged themselves pedophagously.

The children of Alsace are treated around Christmas time (at the feast of Saint Nikolaus, December 6th), to cookies in the shapes of children distributed by Saint Nikolaus (Santa Claus) who is accompanied by Rubezahl, a gigantic man in a mask and cloak, a late impersonation of Wotan, and who can best be identified with Saturn, as indeed can Santa Claus. The one gives the imaged cookies to the good children; the other menaces the bad children. It should be recalled that infant sacrifices and cannibal rites to Saturn survived well into Christian times; in the present rites, unconscious of origins, the ancient rites are sublimated more or less in playfulness.

Ritual is prominently displayed in matters having to do with alimentation. But it covers all aspects of religion, therefore all aspects of life. There is a rule for everything. Man, deprived of instinct, is a habit-former, an obsessional creature. Not only is his language founded upon obsessive reiteration, not only are his dietary manners as well, but likewise his sexual, affectional, social, agricultural, industrial, physical, and learning behavior. In all of these regards, religion and ritual come in the beginning of human existence and remain forever.

If religion persists despite the extensive and eroding process known as secularization, or rationalization, or pragmatization, it will do so logically in the centers of life prone to chaos and accident. That is, religious rites focus upon and persist in the fearful and catastrophe-prone areas and, as from a lantern, diffuse their light perceptibly and gradually into the secular.

For instance, baptism, ceremonializing the creation of new life in the world, is a critical juncture, hence persistently ritualized; the Christian Baptists, who are relatively non-ritualistic and even anti-ritualistic, nevertheless are insistent that baptism into the church should occur by total immersion of the freely consenting new member in water to signify death of the old life and rebirth in the new. Baptism in a church is general among the French, even though the population has abandoned almost all rituals of the Roman Catholic Christian religion. Early Christian leaders believed that they had found in the Deluge of Noah the ultimate precedent and model for baptism, which repeats for each "saved" initiate the end of the wicked world and the entrance into a new epoch.

Rituals are centered upon the creation of the world and man, upon the first time everything was done, upon catastrophic breakdowns of an age and the beginning of new ages, and upon the *rites de passage* of human life - - birth, maturation, marriage, and death. Filling in as important subcategories of these are such features of human existence as warfare, where the gods are the models and the gods "Bless our weapons," as the Kaiser of Germany (and many others) once prayed.

Celebrations of cosmic breakdown are a feature of the focusing of rites upon controlling the world against chaos, as in the case of the Aztecs. The New Year is ignored by no culture, because it stands for the end of one age and the beginning of another; the usual rationalizations are afforded, that harvests are now gathered, that the calendar now repeats itself, etc. Nonetheless, beneath the considerable excitement, stirs the anxiety that the year may not repeat itself, the sun may not turn backwards to reenact the seasons, that once upon a time the world went out of control and could not provide assurances of the repetition of its orderly cycles.

The bacchanalia were orgies named for Bacchus or Dionysus, a god, reputed to have traveled the world with a wild troop of both sexes, carrying wands and serpents, acting out a mad composition of dancing, drinking, battling, sacrificing, cannibalism, and feasting. Regular and sporadic orgies, patterned upon the mythology, persisted for centuries before Christ until the Roman Senate with some success banned them for their flagrant challenge to morality and political order.

The crimes attributed to Dionysus were infinite, yet he received a place on the Olympian council of gods, replacing the gentle Hestia, according to one legend. Dionysus was a sky-god, perhaps originally an errant and destructive comet; the orgiastic behavior accompanying him resembles the kinds of social disorder that have been historically reported upon the fear-inspiring apparition of cometary bodies.

The saturnalia of the Greco-Roman world are more precisely applicable to prehistoric events, when the god Saturn was allegedly overturned in a revolt of his wife and children, particularly Jupiter. The last days of the year are regarded as the period when chaos begins, and the new year is seen as the coming of a new age.

> Even if, as the result of successive calendar reforms, the Saturnalia finally no longer coincided with the end and the beginning of the year, they

nevertheless continued to mark the abolition of all norms and, in their
violence, to illustrate an overturning of values (e. g. exchange of condition
between masters and slaves, women treated as courtesans) and a general
license, an orgiastic modality of society, in a word a reversion of all forms to
indeterminate unity.

So says Mircea Eliade. Types of saturnalia are found
throughout the ancient world - the Middle East, the Mediterranean,
China, Japan, and tribal societies of America. The Hebrew religion is
not excepted, according to Santillana and von Dechend. And they
continue in many places today.

Eliade merges the saturnalia with creation myths. This is
contra-indicated by his own evidence. The catastrophe of Saturn and
the end of its Golden Age involves the destruction of a preexisting,
ante-deluvian, "old world," and therefore comes long after the
original creation.

The dramaturgy of the Babylonian Akitu Festival is illustrative
of "the abolition of lost time, the restoration of primordial chaos, and
the repetition of the cosmogonic act." The god Marduk slays the
dragon of chaos, Tiamat, and creates the cosmos from the fragments
of its body, including man from the blood of a demonic ally of
Tiamat. In the chaos all social forms are confounded, as in the
Roman Saturnalia. It is probable that both creation and recreation are
handled together in the drama; that is, Marduk (Jupiter) is in a sense a
creation god, but the Babylonians and Sumerians had older more
authentic creation gods; Marduk would be, let us way, a recreation
god. Eliade implicitly grants this, when, in discussing the Akitu
drama, he adds, "The creation of the world... is thus retroactualized
each year," and, a little later, "the hierogamy is a concrete realization
of the 'rebirth' of the world and man."

Eliade tends to force all celebrations and rites into *illo tempore,*
"those first great days." He has made an important contribution to
the theory of the history of religions by assembling from all over the
world evidence of the obsessive reiteration in human activities of the
earliest days of mankind. However, he scarcely considers whether real
events lay behind this compulsive return to origins of all peoples, a
mechanism exactly consonant with Sigmund Freud's mechanism of
compulsive reenactment of traumas. Freud, when he essays to explain
the origins of the mechanism, postulates a primordial social crisis
among the hominids, whereby the "father" is killed by the "brothers"

of a horde to gain access to the females whom the "father" monopolized; this theory is so weak, as I have shown elsewhere, as not to deserve treatment here.

Eliade does not offer a theory to explain compulsive repetition of chaos and creation, the most prominent of all ritual behavior. He quotes lines from Jensen's *Mythes et Cultes chez les peuples primitifs* that call out to the original events: "The sacrilege of *not having remembered* is logically expiated by *remembering with special intensity*. And because of its special meaning, blood sacrifice is a particularly intense 'reminder' of this sort." Perhaps relevant as well is an inscription of the tomb of the Egyptian Pharaoh Seti I: "The Light God Ra said: 'You are forgiven your sins. The slaughtered victims remit your extinction.' Such is the origin of the sacrifice of victims."

The shocking psychic fear associated with human creation and the terrors of the active sky can be combined to explain why mankind has persisted, openly or beneath many kinds of subliminatory activities, in reenacting the earliest scenes. But the general catastrophes were several, accounting for the succession of gods, whereas the creation trauma was singular and unique. The human has been responding not only to the successive natural catastrophes which, of course, were also treated as re-creations. In racial memory the traumas blend over time. It is noteworthy that they have not entirely merged, with all distinction erased, but they have apparently merged enough so that on the one hand the historian and theorist Eliade does not separate them chronologically, and so that on the other hand, most creationist scholars who hold to a literal interpretation of Biblical history are preoccupied with the Deluge of Noah, seeing it as the unique catastrophe that sculpted the face of the Earth.

Mankind, in bursting forth upon the Earth, experienced catastrophe, and thereafter was confirmed in his catastrophized memory by a succession of natural catastrophes. His global sense of the sacred, a sense that Otto and others have described as ambivalent feelings of fearful danger and creative power, expanded with each quantavolution of nature and relaxed between the age-breaks.

Rituals are attempts at close encounters with the gods. They are a primary instrument for controlling oneself and the environment as the gods approach. We find the formula quite clearly perceived by theologians who refer to the sacrifice as the use of an intermediary, the oblation, to communicate between the mundane and the divine.

"Sacrifice is ... offered to a divinity in order to establish, maintain or restore a right relationship of man to the sacred order," thus writes R. L. Flaherty in the *Encyclopedia Britannica* article on sacrifice.

The means of ritually controlling the gods (for "communicatio" conveys the subservient theological mood more than it does the aggressive political mood) can be analyzed. They are scarcely exotic, though often esoteric. First, man behaves in imitation of the gods. This is in every sense the same as the behavior of the child with respect to his adult guardian and model. It is intended to gather the strength of the god, and at the same time disarm the god from directing aggression to him. "Imitation is the sincerest form of flattery," as the saying goes. So, if the god fights, the man fights. If the god rages, man rages. If the god bestows generous gifts, so does the man. And so on.

Appeasement of the god's proven potential for aggression against his very worshippers, as well as his enemies, takes many forms. Giving of one's most valued possessions is the most appropriate sacrifice. All manner of bribery, solicitations (it must be discovered what the god wants, even if by trial and error), prostitution (whether as vestal virgins or as temple harlots) - these are common gifts.

Nor does worshipful man stop short of trickery. That god knows what one thinks does not prevent the most ludicrous practicality and flamboyant excesses. "It can't hurt to perform the rites." Do this and that, not because it is right in the eyes of god, but "lest you die;" ritual is to be performed, not understood, nor does it matter to understand. The important thing is to obey the command. Miserliness is common too: "We are not sacrificing at all to Awwaw this year, since rain has fallen early," remarked an Iyala priest of Nigeria, quoted by Paul Radin.

Much of ritual therefore is a kind of tactical game to exploit the gods. The human encountering god is thrown into a panic, He often overcompensates and contradicts his own view of god as all-wise. He will stop at nothing to be on the right side of his god - never mind inconsistencies, preserving other life values, and saving a personal relationship. It is the politics of absolute autocracy to some, to others the politics of a monarchical court with its courtiers, to still others a two-person game, intensely personal.

Without a theory of origins and earliest history, it is perhaps impossible to say whether man modelled kingship upon gods or gods upon kings, whether rituals were practiced among men and then upon gods, or *vice versa*. Our particular theory here would make kingship and politics initially religious and soon afterwards transferred into a partially secular sphere, there ultimately to be pragmatized and secularized.

Later one could have a secular republic such as the U. S. A. or France, highly ritualized with specific rules excluding religion from the rituals. Finally one would arrive at the Marxist republic, the Union of Soviet Socialist Republics and others, where the very permission of religious ritual is viewed as an anomalous and temporary concession. Consistent with its denial of religious ritual, religious faith and revelations are treated as mental aberrations.

Religion without ritual is fear without defences. Secularism without ritual must be the same. The suppression of supernatural belief does not eradicate the existential fear of man but only its referents - gods, spirits, etc.

The French Revolution after 1789 burst upon both the political regime and the church. Churches were seized, the clergy laicized. A great Feast of the Supreme Being was inaugurated, conducted on the Champ de Mars in Paris. It is clear that the Supreme Being was Reason and Nature. Some churches were rededicated as temples to the Goddess Reason, who was sometimes represented by a pretty girl. New rituals were improvised to replace the old ones.

Numerous writers have pointed out that the supernatural is actually irrepressible and finds its way into astrology, "life in other worlds," "the unexplained" (an enlarging, logically boundless area), and the like. Furthermore, the religious finds its way into the divinization of political heroes - "St. Karl Marx," "Comrade Mao," the entombed and preserved Lenin, the charismatic leader Mussolini, or de Gaulle, or Franklin Roosevelt, or Gandhi, et al.

We offer no argument against this line of reasoning. A religion of the supernatural, of faith and of revelation can be educed from such secular social phenomena. We would only wish to supplement them. There may be a reciprocal growth in secular ritual to accompany the loss of religion and its ritual.

Two phenomena accompanying modern secularization display conspicuous growth, and may be surrogates for ritual. One is bureaucracy, the other centralization. The two are interconnected: the logic of bureaucracy tends to centralization. The logic of centralization demands bureaucracy. One sees the shadow of religion and ritual in the two. The French Revolution, anti-religious, gave a great boost to centralized bureaucracy throughout the world.

Centralization is a search for a central truth and law toward which all procedures may be directed. Bureaucracy supplies the procedures. Large-scale armies, mass media, huge building complexes, human and computerized industrial giants, mass transportation, global planning - all of these supply, whatever else they provide (and religion once supplied a distribution system for food out of sacrifices) reiterative, compulsive (compulsory, too), routinized activities lending a feeling of awe and security to those whom they engage and serve.

The idea of "efficiency" is offered frequently as a purely secular notion, an activity that can be carried on without a hint of the supernatural or the rite. In the first place, "efficiency" like "god" is all things to all people, hence is not to be accepted as meaningful at face value. Efficiency as a reduction of activity (energy) between two points (from "here" to a goal) to a minimum is flagrantly contradicted by bureaucracy. Efficiency seemingly contradicts sacrifice and ritual, superstition and magic, but actually religious ritual can and has been over the ages consistently intended to be efficient. The idea is not new; it is only aimed at different goals. One can be sure that ancient priests worked continuously to increase the efficiency of fires on altars.

The orders, rules, and laws, practically all now in written form, which pour out of the ruling organizations of the world, take up many thousands of large volumes a year. Is this not ritualized behavior? It secures those involved from the nagging fear of existence, acting as a lifeline for the weak psyche to grasp. The summary effect of this overwhelming flood of order is to tell people what they must do, and how to go about doing it, in the sacred written word of authority.

Gone for most modern people is the lifeline of religious ritual; in its place is secular ritual. We think of the novels of Franz Kafka (*The Castle, Amerika*) and of George Orwell (*1984*) to illustrate our point. It is untrue, although Dostoevsky wrote so in *The Brothers Karamazov,* and one hears it often said, that "if God doesn't exist, everything is allowed." After all, is it not said of the great Soviet State that "Whatever is not forbidden is compulsory"?

The problem is too large for discussion here. I mean merely to add for consideration that the secularized world has a rich and abundant ritual, as well as secular divinities, charismatic experiences, and supernatural "pastimes" that are more serious than religion to their practitioners. The modern secular child knows more rules than the ancient religious child. And so, too, the adult of this world today. At some stage hereafter we must contrast the two modes of life and evaluate them.

CHAPTER SEVEN

MAN'S DIVINE MIRROR

No god is the same to any two people, nor to any two sects. This is a psychological fact, akin to saying that no two people share the same experience. It would be a more definitive statement if the gods existed in no other realm except the minds of people. It also relates to the fact that no two delusions or hallucinations are alike, although especially when a group happens to hallucinate the same image - an angel, say, or unidentified flying object - the description may be close, and when a mass of separate hallucinations is analyzed statistically, one does obtain averages and types.

When two people discuss a similar religious experience - a visual revelation of the Second Coming of Jesus Christ, say - one can statistically adumbrate shared social and psychic features of the people that tend to qualify them for the experience, such as a deficient formal education, erratic and disturbed personal backgrounds, and so on. Cases where a team of scientific observers, warned and trained to be objective, are rushed to the scene to corroborate the vision are rare.

Even were such to occur, the new (and probably negative) evidence would have to be dismissed on grounds that the preparation for objective identification would necessarily incapacitate the team to share the experience. If the two people had seen a monster in the Sewanee River and called it a dragon and the team had hastened in with cameras and nets, an alligator of a certain size might be captured and the vision placed upon a firm scientific footing. It would not be surprising, then, if the original viewers claimed an improper identification, insisting that the wrong creature had been snared. Whereupon psychologists would once more be called upon.

That gods are often snares and delusions must be admitted. Yet the occurrence of the delusions, we have implied, takes on patterns evocative of actual events and of common mechanisms of the analyzed human mind. Natural expressions of high energy occur in cometary approaches to Earth, deluges of water and other material from the skies, anomalous intensifications of heat and cold by conflagration or sudden icing on a large scale, simultaneous large scale volcanism, and otherwise. Much evidence goes to show more of such catastrophes in ancient and prehistoric times than over the past 2500 years.

We say that the more frequent these occurrences and the greater their intensity, the more that gods appear and the more religious humanity becomes. If these be called gods insofar as they are apparitions and because of their enormous effects, then there is a real historical reason why mankind once was much more religious than now. Geology and archaeology can demonstrate (with much more research than they are inclined to provide) the actual basis for enhanced early religion. Psychology and the history of religion can show how the religious mind has expectedly peaked in these actual stress periods and subsided when the strains relaxed.

Practically all historians of religions and renowned modern theologians have accepted evolutionary theories of cultural development in describing religious history. Even Henri Bergson who spoke of a "discontinuous evolution which proceeds by bounds" saw this progressive achievement of higher forms of behavior against the backdrop of an unchanging natural scenery. To all of such thinkers, religion must have progressed out of a rational advancement of humanity (even though Bergson credits mysticism with innovation in religion). That is, rationally evolving man creates ever more rational religion.

Without correcting the human mental infrastructure, they have placed an ever heavier superstructure upon man, not knowing that when man has assumed the burden of what they term rational behavior, it is because natural conditions have allowed him to do so, and that this happened as much or more during the Golden Age of Saturn as during any period of modern times. Apes have not become smarter; horses have not; how should man have done so without a proven physiological alteration of his mind?

If one wishes to animate the ancient apparitions (metaphorically or delusionally) and assign the fantastically great natural events to interventions of the gods, defining gods as "whatsoever can produce such effects," and further goes on to distinguish and assign gods to the different effects of, say, air, fire, water, and earth, there can be no logical objection. So long as one does not proceed beyond the evidence to impute motives, make misleading classification, and imagine an organization of the cosmos, none of which can be even partly demonstrated, the gods of nature can be said to exist as truly as "democracy" or an "infinite regression series."

Here is where mankind gets into trouble with the scientific authorities of anthropology and psychology: it assigns a great many undemonstrable qualities to the gods and spirits. Then, hardly pausing, it fashions such qualities into a mirror of man, which like the mirror in the fairy tale of Snow White, so long as Snow White is dead, always tells the Queen that she is the most beautiful. The mirror lies.

We can make two principal statements and several dependent propositions about the Divine Mirror of Man: first, all human qualities are found among the gods; second, divine organization portrays a reorganization of the human mind.

To demonstrate that every human quality has been sometime, somewhere, and even frequently, a divine quality requires hardly more than a list of references on the history of religion and anthropology. Let the reader make the test himself; let him try to think of any human action or trait, no matter how trivial or significant, which a god does not exhibit. The humans build a great tower to reach the sky. Very well, the gods have already their sky-topping mountains, their cosmic trees, their pillars of heaven, and many sacred paths by which souls can ascend and angels descend. When the constructions threaten the gods, the gods destroy them. So it happened with the giants who piled Ossia upon Pelion to reach Zeus, who, however, overthrew everything, and as happened with the Tower of Babel, which the Hebrew Lord sent crashing by lightning and quaking.

But this is a sublime challenge, someone may object; an ordinary act is not divine, for example, excretion. But urine is a word from Uranus who copiously watered the earth in earliest times; and gold is the excrement of the gods to some people, perhaps remembering vaguely an exoterrestrial fall-out of the precious metal.

Is the god assembled anthropomorphically? The implication, even when not stated explicitly in sacred scriptures and legend, is that all of the traits of the divine do amount to a creature not unlike man. That Elohim created man in his or their image is, of course, a direct statement of the Hebrew *Genesis,* and if one were to compose a physiological mosaic from all references to Yahweh, the mosaic would evolve to look like Moses and act like him, including how Moses would like to have acted.

The Divine Mirror, it seems, is more perfect than the gazer. For it contains all of his qualities and all of his dreams and desires. Sometimes these are contradictory, but the mirror finds a solution. It may show a god with devilish features, or a god who is both female and male. Does it ever show a god who is both brave and fearful? Often; despite the fact that fear creates gods who are afraid of other gods, afraid of themselves, or mistrustful of their worshiper, this last being a kind of fear that drives gods (as it does men) to excesses of all kinds. So, indeed did the Lord behave toward Job, when the Devil drove him to be suspicious of his devoted and good worshipper.

In an early work, C. J. Jung wrote an *Answer to Job* where, brilliantly but in a fundamentally naïve form, he hints that man is too clever for God. "It were better," however, "not to wax too conscious of this slight moral superiority over the more unconscious God." One notes the marvellous schizoid behavior of the human, Job, when he is trying to control God. The making of the ambivalent god and then the controlling of him becomes the greatest work of man.

God suspects and is jealous of the game that man is playing, a contradiction-in-contradiction, mirror in a mirror in a mirror, contra-contra-contradiction, which the schizoid can continue indefinitely, always one step ahead of God. In the story of Job, one finds the full range of schizophrenic conduct, including the creation of the Lord as the preferred instrument for working out human delusions. I trace the schizotypical character of the human race in other books.

Significantly, wherein lies at least his early naïveté, Jung separately focuses his research upon Job and then upon schizophrenia. In the story of Job and God, we even locate a tendency of humans to make of gods what they would make of themselves if they could, a kind of unreflective healthy instinctive animal, rid of the curse of self-awareness - though this same self-awareness is the only true mark of the human and the source of god as mirror of man.

Usually, it is declared that the gods are not like man, because they possess an infinity of virtues. But who is to say what is virtue, except man-bound-in-culture? And what are the traits that appear infinite in the Divine Mirror but extensions of the valued traits of mankind. Even philosophers, and certainly theologians, submit to the dictates of mirroring when they accept the challenge of defining gods, and thereupon they say god is omni-this and omni-that: omniscient, omnipotent, omnipresent, omnicreative, omnivalent, all-loving, absolutely just, and so on, settling, to be sure, on precisely those qualities that man has and wants much more of: power, respect, affection, wealth, skill, and knowledge.

To win a debate over whether all divinity that man can know is anthropomorphic hardly needs empirical evidence. So logical is the proposition, that it is probably a tautology. That is, granted that man can only know by an extension of himself, the self becomes the model of the real, and no trait can be imagined that is not already present in humanity. Therefore, in the anthropocentric sense, all divinity must be anthropomorphic.

In the days when gods were rampaging upon the Earth, theology was close to the disaster-ridden life of the people, naming and describing the fulsome operations of the divine forces, transmitting direct commands from above, concocting rites, and letting out the chains of fear carefully into sublimatory and practical behavior.

When the gods remove themselves somewhat, the chains are slackened. Language, symbols, and myth are allowed to bury memories deeper. Religion becomes less depictive and denotative, more general and abstract. Finally, philosophy is freed to play about the sacred and rationalize the cosmos. The gods of the philosophers are mirrored. "An otiose God, then, surveying unmoved 'this dusty, fuliginous chaos, ' is the residuum of all this furious apostrophising." So wrote once Frederic Harrison.

We find that the most ancient people - and we are not told how - knew that the planet Jupiter had bands and the planet Saturn had rings. Probably they witnessed them directly and more closely than at any time until the year 1659 A. D., when scientists observed them by telescope. By the time of Plato, several centuries before Christ, this knowledge was perhaps only present in legend, and was part of the legend that has the god Zeus Jupiter overthrowing his father, the god Kronos-Saturn, and binding him to prevent his return to power (and thus bring further destruction upon the world). The knowledge comes to us via the works of the platonic philosopher, Proclus, eight hundred years later (ca. 410-1485 A. D.).

Proclus, in startlingly clear language, but philosophical language, tells us that Jupiter, mighty and powerful, the supreme intellect of the universe, bringer of law and order to the world, asserts his own reason upon the world by putting the also perfect intellect of Saturn under bonds. Then, because Jupiter is logical and just, he binds himself, too, so that he also will be subject to his own ordering principles.

As I proceeded elsewhere to trace the development, the statements of Proclus exemplify how a primordial real experience becomes anaesthetized by its traumatic effects on humans; it is forgotten as direct experience. Yet it is remembered obsessively in the form of a religious creation legend, and then the suppressed memory and the legend are sublimated one more step into philosophy, where they are used to express concepts of divine rule and natural law. The new ideas still give relief to the deep hidden anxieties over the horrible warfare of the gods, and they promote respect for human government and laws, which, it is said, are and should be modelled upon the behavior of the gods.

The nature of the gods is geared into the nature of religious organization. The jealous Yahweh of Moses was not the syncretistic Yahweh of Solomon; nor was the charismatic-leader-led, tribal, confederational, religious organization closely similar to the imperial, bureaucratic, secular-dominated, religious organization of Solomon. Forms of religious organization have been many, no two quite alike as we are prone to say. This, too, is a Mirror of Man. From the organization of spirits-shaman-tribal culture to the organization of the Holy-Trinity-priesthood-Roman Catholic world religion, variation is endless.

The descent of secular organizations from theocratic ones is well marked. For instance, the 13th century forms of political representation in England and elsewhere owed much to the representative convocations of the Dominican Order of the centuries preceding. Where not well-delineated, the lines of descent are concocted. In the 17th century, the Stuart line of England was "demonstrated" to go back to Adam, the First Man, and the divine right of monarchy was sustained. We might begin at the earliest age, and go on for many pages listing the religious structural forms and their secular descendants.

Suffice to say here that the secular forms, so far removed from the primordial religious ones, are nevertheless still "sky-struck." Stars and totems adorn their banners; the right and the left factions stem from the Saturnian Throne in the sky; the official secular calendars are largely religious in origin; the American dollar portrays ancient Egyptian cosmology; parades, processions, decorations, robes and a multitude of rituals precede and accompany officers even after they swear an oath, in which "So help me God" may be absent, but the pledge is as symbolically complete and solemn.

Celestially or mundanely, man is operating with the same mental mechanisms and their external social extrusions. Symbolizing, displacements, identifications, memory, obsession, cognitive disorders, aversion to others - these psychic movements (were they not mostly unconscious, they would be called maneuvers or tactics) are all directed at handling fearfulness, and function in both religious and secular contexts. They are expressed in habitual, orgiastic, catatonic, and sublimatory behavior, which again have religious and secular counterparts.

The reader may have remarked that these mechanisms and expressions are schizoid and, if practiced in full conflict with the customs of one's group, would amount to a full-blown case of schizophrenia. The human is naturally schizotypical - I call him *homo sapiens schizotypus* elsewhere - whether speaking of religious man or secular man; when an individual diverges from the peculiar schizotypicality of his culture, he is identified as schizophrenic.

We would stress how much our view contrasts with the conventional approach, which analyzes the human as a rational individual with egoistic impulses who is struggling to reconcile these with social or altruistic demands. The distinction between self and society is itself a socially imposed distinction as it is presented, say, by Henri Bergson or the English utilitarians (whom he assails). The distinction is *ex post facto*. The *factum* is the schizotypical mechanisms mentioned above. These are what set into motion the operating religious and secular person. The "social" is immediately part of the person; it arises from the original gestalt of creation of the human species, and in the birth and development of every person thereafter.

The experience of all peoples has been generally the same,

intense ecological stresses anciently operating upon a divided, fearful mind. To say therefore that gods are "good" and men are "evil" makes anthropological history impossible, theoretically or as fact. We have already said that gods, relatively or cross-culturally considered, display all "evils" and all "goods." It matters relatively, not absolutely, that the burden of good and evil is shifted to certain different gods, devils or spirits going from one culture to another. The basic facts are the common experiences of "gods" and the ambivalence of the human mind in relation to itself. The ultimate expressions, such as "selfish" against "altruistic," are just that - expressions - not the fountainhead of the social problem or of the problem of man against god.

The obverse to "how the gods could be believed to do evil to people" is, "how the gods could be believed to do good." The efforts of humans to justify the evils visited upon themselves are extraordinary, considering the gravity of those evils. Some profound reason must prevent them from declaring that gods and devils are one and the same - a disaster. Why do they not recognize the animated high-energy forces of the world as the open enemies of the human race? Indeed, this did become finally the feeling of a great many people in modern times, whose change of attitude coincided with a de-animation of the forces of nature.

Primeval man and his successors found good in the gods because in the first place the ideal of the good god itself performed useful functions. The gods created man, and man was superior to the mammals whom he resembled and lived among. Therefore, gods should be loved for their creative deeds.

Still, gratitude is a refined subliminatory trait that would hardly result from this syllogism. There had to arise a satisfying powerful identity out of the gestalt of creation: the creative god was built into the mind of the creature; it was his first projective delusion. His first great relief from fear was placing the responsibility for his creation, not upon himself (an idea that must promptly have occurred) but upon "some himself not himself," ergo a god. Who denied god, denied himself; who denied himself would not survive. The madness of great delusions was the condition for survival.

There remained only the elaboration of the madness into human norms. A quick transfer of traits occurred - man gave to god all of his abilities and took them back as blessed gifts, down to the rudiments of stone age technology, the very fashioning of a club.

Because of the obvious powerfulness of the gods, the gifts acquired power in the human mind, and man would step forward to control the world with an obsessive confidence, a false confidence, very often, yet with enough successes to accredit the transfer. At the same time, man could deny his personal responsibility for all that he was creating.

Further, by imitating the gods, invention was promoted. More and more objects and procedures for controlling himself and others were imagined to descend from the gods and more and more were created under divine inspiration. This despite the interference of the gods thenceforth in inventions of all kinds, wherein nothing could be invented and applied unless it had come from the gods or was blessed by the gods. The psychological mechanism had its drawbacks; in the most peaceful and pragmatic periods, the wellsprings of invention were overlooked, while the subservience of practical innovation and social reforms to religious dogmas and rituals was promoted.

The mechanism for projecting and retrojecting gifts of power and techniques was in itself adequate to explain why a punitive god could be assigned benevolent and beneficent qualities. Yet it was not the only source of the idea of the good god. The first mutant humans came into being in the midst of chaos and destruction. That they had survived while all around them lay a biosphere of death and destruction, including what had been their own kind, was a miracle; their minds were now equipped to reflect upon it.

Mourning was a trait already possessed; mammals and primates mourn. Beyond mourning, however, or if human mourning were to be distinguished, was a new consciousness of the self, an individuation from the group, that could see what had happened to others, see what oneself had escaped, and assign to the escape a selective feature, a blessedness, a sense of being chosen for survival.

Thus arises the quality of personal satisfaction and joy amidst ruin, that interjects itself into the most grandiose human tragedies, and causes people to dance, laugh, and sing when the world shakes and burns around them. It was a primordial human acquisition, directly connected with the animated forces of destruction. Sailors, returning aboard a ship off of Krakatoa in 1883, who watched the desolation of their families on the shore from volcanic explosion and tsunamis, laughed and jumped with joy that they were being spared.

Hysterical conduct, to be sure, in awful fear, but such is the nature of hysteria, and laughter often is a fringe around hysteria.

The divine identification and imitation justified and provided morale for survivors to revive and conquer. A newly-acquired super-mammalian aggression abetted the profits of survival. Those who survived could move out, reinforced by grace of the gods, and in imitation of the gods, readily loot, kill, or enslave whoever remained alive and within range. The material gains of aggression were thenceforth regarded in the category of gifts of the gods, and regularly some portion of them was returned to the gods by means of sacrifices. From old Mexico, Brundage gives us a song composed by the Emperor Axayacatl: "The flower death (for sacrifice and cannibalism) came down to Earth. It came here. It had been created in Tlapallan (Heaven)."

Nor were these the only material benefits that came from the divine delusion. On some occasions, carbohydrates descended from the sky, notably during times associated with terrifying celestial phenomena between 3000 and 3500 years ago, when *manna, soma,* and *ambrosia* were provided to starving survivors. This I explain in *The Lately Tortured Earth,* where too, many legends are reported insisting that copper, gold, silver, petroleum and iron were exploded or dropped onto Earth and used by their finders. Meteoric iron was commonly used long before the controversial "Iron Age" and may have fallen in amounts sufficient to institute this age. Myths of dragons burying gold are met with. And so on. The stone (and wood) age might have gone on forever if the surface of the Earth had not been blasted into metals and by metals from the skies. If this should be a fact, then mankind would be historically as well as psychologically blessed by the gods.

Fountains and springs of water erupted, too, in many places, even where the pre-existing waters had been diverted or buried, so that the gods could be said to have first removed good things and then relented and given them back. The gods, sang Homer, were the givers of all good things. Jupiter took away fire to punish mankind; the god-hero Prometheus stole it and gave it back to man; Zeus enchained and tortured Prometheus eternally for his gift. But the fire remained.

We have spoken largely of displacement, identification, projection, and aggression heretofore. Alongside these mechanisms moves habit, the human's answer to the blunting of instinctive behavior during the creation of self-awareness.

Outstanding in human behavior is the voluntary and unconsciously motivated repetition of actions in every sphere of life. In individuals, the repetition is called habit; in groups, custom. In animals, instinct serves for habit, the distinction generally being that instinct is untrained. Habit and custom are inculcated by training or imitation. Not only is habit pervasive of normal activities of individuals and groups. It is also characteristic of many psychopathologies, where it is called obsession.

The origin of habit and custom lay in the primeval fears of the self-aware human, and the discipline that such fears sub-consciously and later consciously impressed upon him. First came schizophrenic obsession. The more intense a blow or trauma to the body (mind), the more intensely and frequently it is autoinflicted neurologically afterwards. An obsession is an auto-inflicted reiteration of some or all of the initial reaction to a trauma.

An obsession discharges quantas of the stored force of the trauma, which originally could be tolerated short of death only by its redistribution (i. e., memorizing) in successively less related circuitries contacting the affected area. Some effect of a trauma also are discharged through interfering circuitries, some of which were developed in primeval man as analogously obsessive and some in non-analogous behavior, especially symbolic manifestations and erratic uncontrolled seizures.

These forms of dissipating the impactive force of the trauma are founded upon analogous primate behavior. They establish themselves as quasi-voluntary and voluntary activities of the split self, which more or less observes its own reactions and discharges. They are seen by men as voluntary, because the self views the action as a decision of two or more compromising internal selves.

Four major patterns of expression emerged finally from the primeval trauma: catatonic, obsessive, sublimatory, and orgiastic behavior. Authentically human behavior was ever after derived and composed from one or more of these patterns. Hence all human behavior reflects, no matter at how great a distance in time and pragmatic relevance, the traumas of cosmic destruction and creation that made and successively battered primeval humans.

The catatonic consists of activity whose primeval function was to keep the world unchanged. The Atlas who held the world on his back was a catatonic symbol of arrested movement; when Atlas shrugs, the Earth shakes. The Hindu Manu who held the world up for ages while standing on one leg and meditating is another catatonic god. Since the Hebrew god rested on the seventh day of creation and ordered his example to be followed forever, many millions of people have dreaded to violate the Sabbath, fearing that the world would be upset in various ways by the angry God.

Physiologically, catatonism is a freezing effect, to prevent the conscious from opening up blockages of suppressed fear. It acts promiscuously, but also in more sophisticated ways, that is, partially and selectively, reluctantly forced to do so by other more determined modes of coping with the needs of the organism.

Primevally, the person froze with fear. Symbolically, humanly, the meaning of freezing with fear became the preservation, at all costs, of existing circumstances, the arresting of the world, of sense intakes, of outputs, of activity, and especially of free or creative activity, all both individually and socially. By projection, if the person and group stop, the disorderly processes of nature will stop; the disorderly processes are deemed to proceed because people are moving and acting.

Obsessive activity has the function-effect of sustaining a line of behavior, of repeating it endlessly with as little deviation as possible. The first symbols and signs of the self-aware persons were naming and ejaculating. Almost instantly this became liturgy, a continuous repetition - expressive, denotative, and expiatory - of anguish, labelling of the cause of anguish, and formula for control of the cause, all in one utterance, repeated continuously. Thenceforth, over thousands of years, the obsessive in symbol and behavior become infinitely varied and yet basically recognizable as originating in fearfulness and its reciprocal of ritual controls. Habit, "the great flywheel of progress" (William James), and custom came to dominate human affairs.

Sublimatory activity functions and has the effects of discharging impulses that are traumatically aroused, together with associated agglomerated impulses, by deviant behavior that simultaneously and subconsciously is analogous enough to the impulses to be organically tolerated, and yet sends the organism in new directions that not only complement and supplement but also contradict other behaviors. Even when contradictory, the sublimation is subconsciously recognized by others to be providing such discharges and is accepted and even encouraged by them.

Symbolic communication is heavily developed by and originates in sublimatory behavior because it is like an endless treasury of ambiguities, flexible for the most remotely analogous tie-ins of original impulses and ultimate conduct.

Orgiastic behavior functions and has the effects of discharges through explosions of the original traumatic force. It has the characteristics of erratic displays of energy, of spastic behavior, and acknowledged as such: it is actually approved not despite, but because of, its senselessness. It demands death, sacrifices, cannibalism, self-mutilation and the wounding of others - human, animal, plants, property. It is both suppressed by, and revenges itself upon the other patterns of behaviour - erasing obsessions in a burst of destructiveness; alternating with catatonic behavior sometimes side by side; destroying and giving new forms to sublimatory behavior.

The cumulative effect of the four behavior patterns of man was to set him apart as a voluntary self-mover. The continuous gap between the two aware selves allowed a kind of fission-fusion reaction on an energy scale immensely larger and more efficient than that of which animals and hominids were capable. Projects of many different kinds could be generated and carried on. Combinations of the four patterns provided a large variety of model or test cases, the effects of which might be pragmatically adjudged good or bad, before deciding to adopt them as ordinary behavior.

The divine, thereupon, becomes a mirror image of the human, just as schizotypical as, or more so, than man, exhibiting human traits, mechanisms, and expressions. No two minds can see the same image in the mirror. This mirror is emphatically not divorced from human experience. It reflects indeed man's most destructive and exhilarating experiences. All gods are connected with disaster, the greater the god the more central his role in ancient disasters, whose scope is unimaginable to most people today. The primordial human mind governs the modern mind, being the same mind, being retentive of the same experiences.

We presented the view earlier that all religion goes back, overtly or covertly, to the first gods. We presented arguments that mankind was a creation of the very experiences that presented the gods to view. In discussing scripture and legend, we mentioned that the figure of Christ was heavily Greco-Romanized, perhaps even formed for the Gospels by a philosopher-dramatist, Seneca.

The reader may then have wondered: since early Christians had a New Testament, a new model of God and were anti-Jewish (Seneca was so too), why did they not cut their ties with Old Testament Judaism? The reason, I think, is clear: the Christians needed the catastrophic history afforded by Old Testament religion; they required the Creation chaos, the Flood, the harassment of Job, the Tower of Babel, the Destruction of the Cities of the Plain, and the Exodus. Otherwise, they would have condemned themselves to early obsolescence and extinction.

CHAPTER EIGHT

INDISPENSABLE GODS

We have progressed so far from the early chapters of this book that a review of them is probably needed, a final commentary on the divine succession and historical religions. Historical religions conserve the memory of a certain time when the world was created and humans came into being. None says that mankind always existed, or that he evolved mechanically by random association of particles. A purposeful act took place at a certain time. Most religions say that mankind was subsequently destroyed and recreated. Almost always the extermination of humanity stops short at a surviving couple or the equivalent. The subsequent homologue of the first chaos is a subsequent set of catastrophes by flood, fire, wind, and earth movements.

To preserve the memory of the first time of creation is a function of rituals, liturgy, anniversaries, and sacrifices. Many religions have strenuously sought to reproduce, short of deliberately re-annihilating themselves, the exact circumstances of chaos and creation. They have obsessively kept forms, practices, and words that go back to the beginnings of all religion and the first experience with the gods.

All historical religions are therefore highly conservative and weaken their foundations as soon as they admit deviations. The function of inescapable and exactly repetitive practices and symbols is to relieve the massive anxiety stored from the earliest times by confessing what happened in those times and reliving them successfully.

What appears to be radical in religious history is reactionary. Practitioners of the religion, wrought up beyond sufferance, find even the rigid rites of their church insufficient to recapture the moments of chaos and creation. Prophets, apostates, evangelists, and orgiasts arise. So do whirling dervishes and berserkers. They are chiliast or millennialists. They proclaim the end of the world while demanding that everyone acknowledge the full and immediate meaning of the creation of the world. They prepare to die and be saved in the recapitulation of the original catastrophic times.

All historical religions are based upon punitive gods, are self-punitive and are punitive towards others. Gods are adjudged good to the degree to which they refrain from destroying their creatures. Humans exist by divine tolerance. A common word for a good person in most religions in "god-fearing". Personal merit through skills, altruism, and dogmatic belief and practice is sometimes, but more often not, a guarantee to a greater or lesser extent of the gods' benevolence; never is merit a perfect or universal guarantee. This belief in the denial to merit of its due is not, therefore, as some think, a connivance of religion with the envious mob.

Sacrifices are forms of punishment of the self and others to forestall, and therefore to control, a punishment from Heaven. The concept of representation effectively lets a partial sacrifice stand for a full sacrifice and a sacrifice of others stand for a sacrifice of oneself. Sacrifices are said to be gifts freely given; yet it is acknowledged that withholding sacrifices will be followed by divine retribution. The more valuable the sacrifice, and the more strict the rules under which sacrifice and all other kinds of punishment occur, the more pleasing to the gods.

Guilt is self-punishment. It is the refusal of pleasure to some negative degree. We often know it in its late and rather pragmatic sense: guilt is what makes a fickle creature responsible; without guilt, personal and social discipline would be impossible. To get relief from guilt, one follows religious directives or some secularized substitute such as warring for one's country or pursuing "the work ethic."

But primeval guilt originated from the terror of "the other self," the terror produced out of the minute systemic delay of instinctive impulses. At the same time, the heavens were turbulent and terrifying. To control one's unbalanced self, one signalled the gods to arbitrate; and the gods responded, saying, "Your soul is a struggle of good and evil. We, with your cooperation, will take care that the good

dominates you. You are not sick. Be hopeful. Help is on its way."
This formula, although it can be called delusion, was a great
invention. Granted the essential incurability of human
schizotypicality, it alone could lead to a manageable psychic world.

Important anniversaries or holy days are celebrations of divine
destruction and near escape from destruction. Every truly religious
anniversary celebration is therefore ambivalently tragic and joyful.
Anniversary excesses and orgies, at both extremes of somberness and
exuberance, are nevertheless occasions for the relief of tragic
memory, more or less deeply suppressed. Anniversaries cluster
around the great cycles of the ages, which give evidence of having
been common to most of the world's cultures. Calendar diversions,
not psychological changes, have driven apart the anniversaries of
different cultures; they are farther apart in days than they are in mind.
The end of the year inspires saturnalia in many cultures. Also thus,
Roman Catholic and Greek churches mark a different Easter holiday
for unessential reasons. Anniversaries sometimes are pulled together
in a given culture by their original proximity during a cycle, such as a
solar year, and by their psychological resemblance. Thus, Venus
(perhaps at -3437 B. P., where Before Present =1984 A. D.) and Mars
catastrophes (perhaps in -2671) occurred around March 23, close to
the Spring equinox; the holidays were merged ultimately, and are
submerged at Easter time in Christendom and comparable holidays
in other cultures.

Sublimation, like ritual, is universal in religion; it pacifies,
dissembles, represents, and rationalizes the strict conditions of the
fatal times. Sublimation becomes more secular and pragmatic with
the evaporation of stored anxiety over long periods of prosperity and
peace. Disaster, deprivation, and frustration raise anxiety levels; they
cause reactions against secular sublimation occurring in the artistic,
social, political and religious spheres; these activities are attacked as
irrelevant and blasphemous.

Furthermore, all religions incorporate directives for every
aspect of life - work, sex, property, power, relations, health, and
knowledge. Humanity was created and made deistic at the same time;
the human mind is not logical, but it is wholly occupied by a way of
looking at the world as a supernatural creation. The question of
separating special values and calling these "the province of religion"
has no meaning to a mind that was originally formed with every value
at stake.

Religious practices are basically similar everywhere and have been from the start. Permutations of practices are innumerable. The new humans executed religious observances among their first acts. In this sense, all the world's religions came from one religion, that of the first and only band of humans. Then different experiences befell the different peoples. Some were non- catastrophic experiences and these brought many minor changes. Other experiences were catastrophic -- global and intense -- and these reinforced the basic resemblances of religions while at the same time prompting many minor variations. Thus ultimately, history came to witness a similar succession of great gods ruling amidst a congeries of ethnic religions.

One god has been replaced by another on various occasions. Almost always, the replacements wa successful because of unconscious techniques of cross-identification and rationalization. Sometimes men sought to replace gods by deliberate choice, with or without the help of events such as cultural amalgamation; invariably then compulsion and heavy propaganda were employed. Such occurred when Hinduism moved over Southeast Asia, when Christianity came to dominate the Roman World, and when Islam moved across Asia and Africa.

The replacement of all gods by materialistic and atheistic ideology is a special case, discoverable, in non-catastrophic times, among philosophical schools such as the ancient cynics, among scientists and humanists of the post-enlightenment, and among communists.

Invariably secular replacers have argued the lack of empirical proof of the existence of gods; they have also stressed the contradictions of ruthlessness and mercy in the concepts of god; and they have attacked the behavior of religious establishments. As alternative behavior they have recommended principles of brotherly love, cooperation, and mental health, among humans, or principles of an ideally organized state that provides enough goods to satisfy people's needs without recourse to supernatural agents.

The major proof that such ideologies might succeed is based upon the waning of the gods when societies possess a pragmatically optimistic morale and are materially prosperous or believed to be potentially so, as recently. Then the gods have seemed remote and unneeded; considerations of logic and efficiency would appear to dictate their abandonment, removal, and forgetting.

Even under optimal conditions of prosperity, secular morale, compulsion and propaganda, the replacement has proceeded slowly and painfully. At the peak of their success, the ungodly ideologies have been undermined by new gods (e. g., Christianity in the Roman Empire), resisted successfully by the masses (e. g., communist Poland, 1945-1983 A. D.), transformed into secular religions of temporary duration (e. g., Roman Emperor worship, *der Führer* Hitler, Comrade Lenin), or transformed into pseudo-scientific therapeutic or philosophical sects employing substitute semi-divine agents (e. g., gurus, anthroposophists).

The fundamental obstacle to ungodliness has been the construction of the human mind. Inasmuch as the events of creation that split the hominid character introduced the splitters as gods, humans become god-seekers as part of becoming human. The particular manner in which the universe was seen for the first time implied perforce the instrumentality of divinity. Self-awareness, symbolism, and projection, driven by fear and memory, formed a nature which was unceasingly prone to discover gods.

Far from being an afterthought, the gods were a first thought. To excise this thought, after thousands of years of experience with it, was not only most difficult pragmatically; it was structurally impossible, at least as long as the origins, function, and mental structure of religion were not understood.

To forget the gods is impossible; the memory deck can only be reshuffled. To retain self-awareness without schizotypicality is a contradiction in terms. Human creation involved a basic reconstruction of mammalian mind; to extinguish this essential schizotypicality would restore man as an instinctive mammal, but is in any event now physiologically and psychologically impossible. Symbolism as the effect of the split self, flows naturally and cannot be obliterated. By the same logic and dynamics, treating symbolically with both the "other self" and the "outsider-others" must inevitably result in projectional thought, that is, treating the "outside other" with the same mechanism and feeling that the self utilizes in dealing with its "own other."

All of this process is transactional and the transaction is of the essence of human being. Therefore a group mode of projection, a group communication, is inherent in the individual-social complex. Thence, naturally, whatever is unanswered and questionable becomes a matter for resort to authority - that is, a prevailing, preponderant group opinion. Since the group is forever under historical and existential stress, it is forever seeking authority and incapable of receiving satisfactory answers to its questions without a symbolic, abstract and animate referent that provides solution. Thus it happens that, if humans exist, god exists. God is the closing of the circle - both question and answer. But so inextricable are the question and answer that only logical artifice can distinguish and designate the two.

Man's need to control the terrible and the terror causes him to invent gods. Nowadays, if one were asked how to control or stop an advancing comet, he would dismiss the possibility, and say that we must await it. He is not prepared to undertake all the actions that ancient man had ready just for such approaching catastrophes - propitiation, sacrifice, ritual, saturnalia, "going on the warpath." Nevertheless, as catastrophe approaches, at first slowly and then rapidly, and then hysterically, the modern human will act like his ancestors, including the excesses of guilt for not having foreseen the deserved end of all folly. He will draw upon the dwindling and remaining reserves of the "old time religion."

If the fossil voices telling us of the nature of the gods and of the rules for man's behavior respecting the gods are distorted and incorrect, and though they are not valid and reliable guides, yet these voices have told us things of positive value. They have given us foundations of history. They have recounted the basic facts of existence repeatedly. They have conjured existences differing from ours. They have in effect performed innumerable experiments with the allegedly divine from which we can learn what not to do religiously, and to a lesser extent what to do.

Perhaps the greatest lesson they have taught us (by negative inference) is that the religion of today and tomorrow should not be sought in the religion of the past: that humans, until they reach some certain level of perfection, cannot be trusted to have known and arrived at the nature of the gods. Whenever historical man has said "Let us change our religion," (even if he does so in the name of preserving the old religion) he is saying "We were wrong about god and religion and it is up to us now to find a new way to god and a new religion."

The gods have retired into new forms, but they still operate through the busy humans whom the poet Rilke called "the bees of the invisible." The gods are still everywhere and are not as remote as our scientific texts would have us believe. They are in astrology, in magic, in fortune-telling; they fly to the scenes of disaster; they augment the forces of authority; they heal and console; they scare; they make anxious; they set the rituals for a multitude as they have done since the times of Ouranos.

They assume their own negation: for they argue with themselves in Natural Law, Bureaucracy, in Dogmatic Materialism, in Reified Words, in Mummified Heroes, in Times and Worlds without End. They let themselves be moulded into One and the One obliges his necessities by becoming Many. Beyond all else, they stand at ease waiting for Armageddon and the Day of Judgment. Then they will don their armor and gather their hosts.

Although they have retired, it still takes rare courage to contemplate all of their continuing manifestations and to resist the invention of new negations. There is yet nowhere else to go and few who would follow.

By skimming along on the thin ice of the cerebral cortex or by mathematical astrophysics or metaphysics or another such exercise, the gods can be sublimated. Dumb bestiality may be equally functional. We think that of all ways of facing them, the best is to look at them everywhere, contemplate their every manifestation, anticipate their reappearance, but do no more. If there is any question of human madness, it is erased when one pretends to be divine. Our human destiny is an open question. We deny our humanity if we try to close it. We belittle ourselves if we plead with the gods to answer the question at any cost.

Whenever gods and religious practices have been abandoned, put aside, forgotten, changed consciously or unconsciously, those who made such changes are saying to us their descendants, "Do not think that our ancestors, or us, or even you, will have the answer. There will be New Testaments without end." We the present generation are told that we are not the first, nor the last, but a truth-seeking figure in the series of forevers until the day when somehow, somewhere, we shall be perfect. At which time, we might, if we dared, claim omniscience, omnipotence, and the fullness of virtue.

In hastening to accuse traditional religion of claiming falsely absolute truth and morality, we often fail to see in the seeming absoluteness its inherent self-confessed contradiction. Just as psychiatry has proven that excesses of anger, self-destructiveness and aggression have ordinarily come out of self-doubt and self-hatred, so we can see in the madness and excesses of historical religious behavior the same psychological sources of self-doubt and self-hatred transformed into dogma, authority, bigotry, punition and guilt in the name of absolute achievement and arrival at the nirvana of perfection. Yet even while civilizations and peoples are being destroyed in the name of absolute truth, newly arrived at, a class of readers or priests of the absolute are contradicting the behavior in gushes of explanations and interpretations of the ways of the gods. As the Hindu Brahmin calculates, the warrior slays. As Anselm seeks proof, Kings crusade.

The most important question of religion is not how to eradicate gods, but to establish gods at one with humanity and the human soul. For there can be no logical or moral objection to the concept of and belief in gods in themselves; again the human being, insofar as he knows any happiness, has known it in activities of a sublime sort that are inextricable from the divine. A formula and model is required, which is physically possible, and which will forego conflicts of the self, among humans, and between devils and gods. Specifications are: a) sufficient relief from fearful stress to permit the search for a new formula; b) a search for physico-chemical change agents (whether mutational or continuously operative) that would eliminate terroristic memories, with all that subtends from such in the way of self-destructiveness and other-destructiveness without damaging, and optimally while promoting, the affectional and inventive facilities of humans; c) and, while the search goes on, and anticipating that the search may be unsuccessful, the invention of social strategies (therapies and institutions) that will hold the conflicts in abeyance indefinitely.

Secularism is a negative counterattack against religion, justifiable as a restraint against malpractices known to everyone. Generally, however, humankind is not in a state to abandon religion and the gods. At best it is capable of achieving a concerted view of an overall divinity and the sacredness of existence. It can borrow from and encroach upon science. Great good would ensue, provided that the concerted belief could work its way into the aims and practices of myriad rituals of human lives.

Part Two

THEOTROPY

Whatever is failings, past and present, mankind continues to pursue religion. Even when most intent upon relieving himself of its falsehoods, constraints, and burdens, he exudes the divine and the supernatural, and these coagulate into habits and practices definable religious.

There are three causes of this incessant and probably inevitable theotropy. One lies in the delusional structure of the human mind, which must exist in the supernatural no matter how it may transform its perception into operations of abstractions and logic.

A second cause of religion rests with the potent limitations of mankind, who has learned that much more than himself and his activities occupies the universe, a something that may be immeasurably greater in its goals and influence.

The third cause of theotropy is the human need to expand his sphere of inquiry. One cannot rest where one is; one must forever seek to expand – in effect, then, to divinize oneself. No ending in defeat is allowabl, no surrender to entropy. Theotropy, as much or more than entropy, is the rule of the universe.

In this inescapable commitment to religion there is little which connects to the problems of ordinary ethics.

Good and bad are the bickerings of passengers on a train rushing through the night. And the consolations of religion are the resolutions of these bickerings in all the compartments of all the classes of all the cars. Religion here is peaceful accommodation which rarely succeeds and never fully succeeds.

The real religion, or call it theotropy, does less for one than one longs for, but ever more for one and one's kind towards an indeterminate destination. We do not know where we are going, but we are making better speed.

CHAPTER NINE

SACRAL VS. SECULAR MAN

Any old religion is likely to have a complete life-program, guaranteed to give satisfaction. It will include answers to all problems that arise, with a counselling service from birth to death. This is no mean achievement, but rather a work of unceasing genius characterizing all ages and all cultures, and therefore thousands of designs and operative systems. Our admiration of the astronomical universe pales in the light of universal religiousness. Indeed, if one is hungry for proofs of the existence of ultimate design and intelligent gods, here is fertile ground to plow.

But why, out of all this experience has there not occurred one religion of all times and places for all people, such that a model human being would lead a happy life? Why should not one formula have been discovered? Why all the changes, conflicts, misery? In replacing the instinctive existence of other creatures, why could not man rapidly invent just that proper set of behaviors that would satisfy the respective and combined needs of his human mechanisms, and culminate in expressions of satisfactory existence? Is there some practical impossibility, the fault of the external world? Or is there some inherent contradiction of the mechanisms of human nature?

Let us set up a model of a religious citizen (not a leader) and inquire whether he should be happy, and, if not, why not. We call him "sacral man," not because he is sacred, but because he believes a great many phenomena and actions are sacred. He sacralizes.

A thorough moral defence of religion from the standpoint of its expression through sacral man has not appealed to modern writers. Such old and religiously circumscribed works as Bunyan's *Pilgrim's Progress* will hardly do for these days, when the field instruments of sociology, biology, psychology, economics and political science need to be orchestrated for the purpose. Available are negative critiques of ritual and assaults upon the supernatural. But where are the moral scientific (as opposed to merely sociological) studies of the Baptist and the Secularist living on the same street, multiplied a thousandfold to cover the world scene?

The ideal sacral person is born of religious parents, is baptized at an early age, and attends schools whose curriculum and teachers are of same belief. He or she hears of the gods, and experiences religious rituals, at an early age, so that by the time of receiving catechism he is already identified with supernatural beings and is pleased to learn that they have played the most important role in all major and many minor events of the history of his culture. Well before receiving formal religious instruction, he has been rewarded and punished in the name of the gods, and (he is convinced) by them directly. He knows this latter to be true, because he has had indirect and accidental rewards and punishments at the hands of what "must have been god." He has a fairly concrete impression of at least one god, the Great God, anthropomorphic but dressed in ritual clothing. He knows of many instances in which God has intervened in the current lives of persons dear or near to him, and to many others that have been the objects of his affection or the attention of his closely identified mentors.

Following upon years of catechism, he can explain events by himself to the satisfaction of members of his religion, and possesses a general history of his group and of mankind from their earliest creation by his gods. He can sacralize readily, that is, impute sacred meaning to any event, natural or human, consistent with his religion. His religious mentors have long since informed him of the great political climate of his larger culture respecting his religion, so that he can know what to expect from strangers in and outside of his culture.

He knows how to invoke the gods by prayers and rites, even only by mentation and, perhaps with a poor sense of statistics, believes his score of successes far outnumbers his score of failures.

He enjoys a logic that employs heavily the formula, "This follows That because God willed it;" "God must have willed This" (where 'This' is an event with significance and within the expected scope of God's actions - love - death, etc., or so unusual as to be the work of God); "This other cannot be, because God would not will it."

He questions authority, since he is early forewarned of its religious untrustworthiness. He pursues a line of secular work regularly and responsibly, as an offshoot of religious ritual behavior. He understands readily the news of the larger world, for there is a general correlation between his political and religious friends and enemies. By virtue of his early training in displacement and projection, he can readily conceive of the larger society, even the whole world's people, within the sphere of and dependent upon his gods. His sources of mundane authority, if not religious, partake of the respect, authenticity, and reliability granted religious authority.

Births, marriages, accidents, careers, illnesses, and deaths of all with whom he identifies - who are part of him - are handled by old, well-known procedures. He is probably better able to confront a personal disaster by appropriate sacred explanations, instead of trying to cope with it independently as, for instance, does the character Charlotte, in Joan Didion's novel, *A Book of Common Prayer*, who, highly secularized but also fearful of self-examination, slips into catatonic denial and mourning when it develops that her daughter was pursuing another life, an *alter ego*, of political criminality. For sacral man, ways and limits of mourning are well-set. Reactions and decisions are pre-fabricated.

He can feel secure that all happens as part of a sacred history, elevated to celestial levels of meaning, and contemplates and suffers his own death in the same frame of mind. Since he identifies with gods, his time scales for personal achievement and for the expected future history of the world, including even rewards and punishments for actors on the present scene, are celestial as well as according to the secular calendar. He is confident of indirect and unknown measures being taken on his behalf by supernatural agencies.

From early childhood, he has been god-fearing. By satisfying the gods, he is exempted from much fear of men and accidents: "If I please God, God will take care of me;" "When God calls, I am ready to go." He realizes very early in life that he has problems of self-control; he projects the unruly selves onto the deities, and thus can "bargain with them at arm's length. Self-hate becomes devil-hate.

When his psychic system becomes well established, he acquires self-confidence.

He has several persisting problems. Some are due to his inherent structure as a human being. Others are owing to his uniqueness when confronted by what must, after all, be a general formula of his religion for handling all humans. There occur also conflictful features of his larger culture, and accidents and natural disasters. Thus his religion, so holy to him, may be disliked by other groups with whom he must deal. He (and his group) may have such consistently bad luck with nature that active punitive measures are continually taken - prayers, sacrifices, guilt, fasting and abstentions. Aggressive behavior against outsiders is sometimes called for by prophecy and divination: "God needs help in punishing his enemies."

Furthermore, he may be genetically a "difficult character" for his religious institutions, a "nervous type" uncontrollably impatient with ritual, a person whose parents were a little deviant and unwittingly made him more deviant from the religious norms of belief and behavior. Guilt-feelings, suspisciousness, self-destructiveness, extravagant behavior (aggressiveness, asceticism, etc.) may result.

Finally his modes of logic may interfere with what he wants to do with himself and the world. If the gods manage so much, he is left to cope with little, and may see little need for pragmatic learning. He may, by continuous resort to his religious logic, become stupid and retarded in contributing to and gaining from the larger culture, where different logics are called for, such as "This cannot occur without That" or "To obtain That, do This" and no more. He may suffer from a great many floating opinions, unanchored to mundane cause and effect, good for ritual, useless for practical life, whether dealing with people or tools.

Regarding these issues as a whole, one large risk seems to confront model religious citizens. The near impossibility of a general religious system being all things to all people all the time causes universal individual problems within the religion. It also causes divisions into priesthood and parishioners, mystics and ritualists, managers and managed, and so on, which aggravate the insecurities of all affected by the divisions, that is, of all believers. Ritual resembles instinctive behavior and may cover most aspects of life except revelation. No religion exists without a place for mystic revelation. Yet revelation is the opposite of ritual. Somehow every church must give birth to and nurture this hero (or assassin).

In addition, every religion exists within at least a partially secularized society; even in the most simple tribal society, where all seems to be definitively sacralized, there is an everyday need to confront and exploit nature, to use tools variously, to deal with outsiders. Conditions change; religion is conditioned; religions change. Every ritual change is a slap in the face of the religion, and face-saving tactics are numerous.

I am not taking present Western European society as typical of religious settings, for this would be too easy. Change and secularization are rampant. I am trying here, as elsewhere in this study, to employ the most conservative type of analysis, and to avoid taking advantage of the many loop-holes of speculation and illustrations that religious history and philosophy ordinarily profit from.

I am asking consideration of a relatively changeless culture, while asserting that there is never a state of changelessness. And so, within and outside the model citizen, change is happening and causes him lifetime anxieties which the religion cannot possibly control by scripture or rites.

A calculus of felicity is not difficult to imagine. The greater the stresses within the church and in the relations (direct and indirectly effective) between the church and the environment, the greater become the anxieties and uncontrollable outbursts of our model citizen; the greater then the changes within his groups as well.

In none of this discussion have we spoken of the moral values of the activity, except we have presumed a kind of *dolce vita religiosa* for the citizen. We have not asked how many orphans has he sheltered, how many cannibal feasts has he enjoyed, or how productive has he been, nor have we made any quantitative gauges of his feelings of nearness to god.

It seems that we must always come up to the point where we are saying "What his religion happens to say is good, is in fact good." whereas we know "in our hearts and minds" that this cannot be. There has to be more than this to justify a religion on moral grounds. Is there some metaphysical morality that can weed out bad from good religions, bad from good citizens?

Or, perhaps, a model of secular man can reveal, by way of contrast, a morality overshadowing religious morality. Let us see. As with sacral man, we shall be taking an optimistic view of his development; the model is optimistically biased. Here now the person we have in mind begins life as the child of parents and in a group who disbelieve in the supernatural and practice no rites in the name of gods or spirits. They point out to the infant actions and persons whose effects are good or bad. The child is taught that nothing exists unless it can be experienced by himself and proven to his authorities, for he has these, too, in his parents and attendants. He is trained to reason pragmatically rather than to practice religious rituals or seek revelations.

He is ritualized, but in the name of necessary training to achieve good or logically necessary effects. By reward and punishment he is taught to seek or avoid objects, persons and activities that he is likely to encounter. He is discharged from training when his own sense of right and wrong appears to rule him adequately.

He learns that his society is benign in its intentions toward him, behaves justly toward him and others, and protects him from himself, potential assailants, and foreign enemies. If he participates voluntarily in his own training, he will acquire skills that the economic system and the governments will welcome and pay him to use.

Ritualized or routine training is justified in terms of its consequences. As the British Statesman Gladstone put it (1876) in the years when the concept was becoming current, "The Secularist.... does not of necessity assert anything but the positive and exclusive claims of the purposes, the enjoyments, and the needs, presented to us in the world of sight and experience."

There is only body, not soul (except metaphorically), and no afterlife to look forward to or worry about. He may enjoy fictional stories about the supernatural; he may pretend "for fun" that any phenomenon is unreal. He observes a number of secular holidays arising out of political, social, and heroic events.

His respect for scientific method (empiricism, facts, logic, experiment, control of the environment) is high; he claims to believe only in its application and findings, whether in the human or the natural realm. He expects a continuous upgrading of his life, partly because of a general upsurge in health and living standards. His feelings are not rigid nor profound, He expects every person to do his duty, and does not accept authority without explanation in material, empirical, and logical terms. He seeks generally to belong to groups whose leaders are elective.

What will be our felicity calculus for such a model citizen? He may be on the whole as "happy" as the religious citizen. The word "happy" would mean a usual mild euphoria, which, we must admit, may come genetically, or as a result of brute affection generously granted the infant being. Still, this affection may be tendered by his identification with "Infant Jesus" in certain cultures, which would therefore allow an intrusion of religion even into the recesses of infancy.

What he loses of the security in the perceived protection of the gods, he makes up for by an increase of security owing to the perceived way in which changing explanations go along with changing events. His defences stop at the grave, but his hopes of increased beneficial effects of science for himself and his human identifiees are greater.

He has fewer judges of his actions, and perceives fewer entities to please. He will, however, be more frequently and poignantly disappointed with humans, because their conduct is not mediated through his gods, and strikes him directly and rudely. His only hope is other humans. This increases his load of fear and anxiety, and probably this will be heavier than the fear-load of religious man.

His temperament may also be more mercurial. On one hand, his life offers less inspiration and may be insipid, while on the other hand he may strain for sensory stimuli and orgiastic behavior. He is not likely to be less aggressive or less vicious than religious man.

His morality is no more explainable than that of religious man. He simply holds it on natural grounds: "That is the way people behave when they are not driven by superstition or authority."

The secularization of modern times may well have had its likenesses at certain times and among certain groups of the Golden Age of Saturn, the Confucian period of China, the Middle Bronze Age in the Near East, the Classical age of Greece, the pagan Roman Empire, the Renaissance, and other eras. The clash between the religious and the secular is prominently displayed. We have an idea that a large section of the elite, at least, in these eras was a disbeliever, a shopper for ideas, luxuriating in freedoms of choice among supernatural views and between cultism and materialism.

Here may be the difference - freedom of choice against a bound-up cosmos, not secularism *versus* supernaturalism or religion or sacralism. We cannot be certain at all that the secular man has ever been really secular, rather than merely a disintegrated sacred man.

The modern secular man was emerging in the Renaissance. Machiavelli was living at the same time as Saint Ignatius of Loyola (1491-1556), founder of the Jesuit order. Loyola, unlike the author of the *Prince,* who moved fully and confidently into the modern disintegrated secular society, was seized by the need to keep the total image of Jesus under control and in mind, and to capture and reintegrate any escaping impressions and thoughts. Roland Barthes has grasped the essence of Loyola's mission and procedures, as spelled out in Loyola's book of *Spiritual Exercises.*

> The obsessional character of the Exercises blazes forth in the accounting passion transmitted to the exercitant: as soon as an object, intellectual or imaginary, appears, it is broken up, divided, numbered. The accountancy is obsessional not only because it is infinite, but above all because it engenders its own errors... [Every failure induces, requires, more accounting.] Everything is immediately divided, sub-divided, classified, numbered off in annotations, meditations, weeks, points, exercises, mysteries, etc. [That is,] The Exercises can be conceived as a desperate struggle against the dispersal of images which psychologically, they say, marks mental experience and over which - every religion agrees - only an extremely rigorous method can triumph.

The whole aim and process is a totalitarian domination of the mind for the purpose of putting oneself into a position to ask God questions and to receive passively the answers. All vagaries were returned to the Source. There is no denying the social impact of the Jesuit method and practice. Allowing that traditional Catholicism continued inertially, Jesuitry became a great active sword that held much of secularism at bay while causing it to involute.

Evidence abounds that secular man is actually a form of sacral man with Jesuitical control. What is sacred possesses for its experiencer an aura of the holy, of awe, of fear, of divine arbitrariness, of supernatural animation. Sacral man in his extreme expression sees the cosmos and all its details as sacred; there are few of such men, of course. The extremely secular man sees everything as void of the supernatural and fully accessible to the senses; there are very few of such men, too.

Let us provide some categories of behavior that might be regarded as sacred or at least non-sensible, to which most so-called secular men adhere. For one thing, they believe in many myths, myths of their descent and families, of their country, of the history of their locale, of wars and voyages. More, and now we make a few specific allusions applying to some, by way of illustration, they hold myths about GM, GE, IBM, their President and political leaders, Albert Einstein, Hollywood, the Mafia, the flag (" Old Glory"), Harvard University, the "Spirit of Saint Louis," the Philadelphia Eagles Football Team, Bellevue Hospital, the "Monopolies," "Justice," "free will," "reason," "truth," "nature," snakes, elephants, diets, and so on and on.

What do we mean by associating such people first with myth, then with the supernatural, hence with the sacred? The myth has in common with the sacred a non-empirical aura of "emotion" or feeling attaching itself to a non-existent or otherwise psychologically incomplete perception such that, whatever it is, it would not recognizably exist unless it were mythified. International Business Machines (IBM) does not exist as entity, but only as hundreds of millions of mental and physical operations of people, partly related to machines. But "it" is "mighty," "global," "venerable," "rich," "progressive," "losing money this year," "in need of revitalization," and so on. One is "loyal" to it, "depends" upon it, "accepts its policies," "questions it sincerity," "sues it," tries to "break it up," "ignores its complaints" and so on. Lawyers hop around on "its giant body like fleas on an elephant," "defending it," "justifying it," and of course "living off of it."

A great many people derive a feeling of the supernatural and sacred form when functioning in the corporate ambiance. The Chief Executive of the great Schlumberger multinational enterprise said recently that a corporation nowadays must learn from the Japanese that "we have the responsibility that religion used to have."

Are these behaviors and beliefs any less religious, say, than the behavior of believers in a volcano religion? The typical secularist worships a dozen such volcanoes; he is polytheistic; he believes in the supernatural and practices rites in regard to it. I do not argue here the consequences: this mythicized aggregate produces millions of hard objects for people; what does the religious aggregate produce but "useless objects" such as church buildings and a superabundant "software?"

We cannot maintain that secular man is less superstitious than sacral man. Does he more often believe "13 is an unlucky number" or carry a rabbit's foot for luck? Encyclopedias of false beliefs and superstitions are available, but they do not speak to this issue. Superstition is sacralization gone wild, uncontrolled by formal religious authority or science. There is very little difference, too, between superstition and the "false cause" of an anxiety; worrying over the number 13 is not much different in cause and effect than worrying that the airplane in which one is sitting will plunge to earth. Secular man has a plethora of both types of illnesses.

Inseparable from myth in practice are symbols and fictions. Language is but the greatest set of all fictions. That it is magical is provable in the behavior of humans in regard to it from their beginnings up to the present. Words lead a life of their own, in the world of words, distinct in part from the objects to which they ordinarily refer. Modern secularists use words freely; a candy is "divine;" every accident is a "catastrophe." No matter; that the world turns with an energy of 10^{37} ergs of energy does not deny to a leaf wafting down from a tree its own erg. What we have in secularism is a disintegration of the sacred cosmos into infinite particularistic ergs of the supernatural, but at the same time a denial of the cosmic supernatural.

Words merge into symbols, which may be words, pictures, displays, but also contain the impact of sets of words, without integration with the grammar of the language. A symbol contains a stimulus to arrive at an attitude or predisposition of mind or behavior. The symbol of the cross has been found throughout the world from the time of the earliest gods up to the present, denoting the chief god or a reference and extension of the god. Wherever a cross occurs, the supernatural does as well; in the ancient world, stones of Hermes were put up at crossroads. Many symbols are likewise ancient. Some of them, like the cross, find their way into the secular crests of noble families, secular institutions, the trademarks of modern corporations, and the escutcheons of government agencies.

Such modern references are very weak, it is said; this is true, and art designers and public relations experts will invent trademarks and other symbols for a price, using scientific techniques for determining how readily the public will recognize and accept the symbol. Still, unauthorized use of the trademark can incite a law-suit for millions of dollars; something sacred must be conveyed. It contains more than a single erg of the supernatural.

So it is with fictions, which are of several kinds, including the words, myths and symbols referred to already. We need only to mention that others remain, and also contain qualities of the supernatural, and they are continuously and necessarily employed by the secular mind. The "average" is one of the most useful concepts of science, but it does not exist. Very often sought, like the Golden Fleece, once found, it leads to marvellous gains. That "everyone knows the law" is a fiction treated as fact in a court of law; "ignorance of the law is no excuse for an offense."

Science, law, literature, drama, and music constitute a veritable fictional world that no amount of secularism can eradicate. Secular man can only claim that these are all piecemeal tools, that he "uses" them, that they do not make him a believer in the supernatural, and that he can understand me when I tell him that these are unreal. But this must be a very special secular man, not an ordinary one, for the ordinary one does not see the dizzying use of hundreds of tools; he is used by them, attaches all kinds of fleeting supernatural associations to them, and does not understand well at all when I speak of them as unreal.

So the ideal, extreme, purely secular man will try to squeeze out of life all that is fictional, we suppose, if it ever ended in anything but the most mad hermeticism, with various rituals for exorcising fictions, in a direct confrontation of the real. Pure secularism would be a life of instinctive stimulus-response: wordless, thoughtless, myopic, and solitary. Wrung out of existence would be the arts, politics, law, the market-place, love, human relations, and science itself, including both the conception of all these and all of their ritual accompaniments.

Since he must himself employ the supernatural and its rituals, secular man, we see, does not so much want to destroy religion as he does to particularize it, to make it pantheistic and kaleidoscopic. He wants to keep all his options. He wants full freedom to pick up and lay down any iota of the supernatural or any practice connected with it. He is like the sophisticated Roman of 2000 years ago who also wanted to pick up and lay down any god or rite as he pleased. He does not wish to be part of an all-embracing and integrated cosmic religious system, nor even to be reminded that everything in the world and in culture is tied to everything else, even secularly, if not sacrally.

Religion as such threatens his options. He wants to freely disperse his affects and attentions. He wants to be free to change them. He admires the composer who builds idiosyncratic tonal works or the sculptor whose "Composition in plastic, number 18" pretends to communicate with nothing or nobody. Just so, he wants individually to compose and recompose the vignettes of his life.

There is accordingly a strong trend toward the disintegration of morality. Morality, too, is piecemeal in secularism. Each item is judged right or wrong by itself. We note this in pragmatism where the consequences of an act determine its morality. We note it in American law where social consequences tend to be the measure of a crime and its punition. We note it in the press, where instantaneity and shocks push aside moral priorities. We note it in democratic politics, where the politicians must, and willingly do, fix the plight of whoever is complaining most, generally ignoring the "good of the whole," scales of values, or long-term considerations: "The wheel that squeaks gets the grease."

Still, the supernatural of everyday life in modern society is not enough religion for a great many secularists and they solicit new religions, inventing them, so they think, actually "reinventing the wheel" time and time again. These are by no means to be dismissed; they are heroic endeavors to join science and traditional religion, to worship the Divine and the Good without reference to the succession of gods, to build peaceful humanistic communities, to make contact with presumably intelligent beings in outer space, to achieve sacred communities with new rituals that dignify rather than abase their members, and to build a satisfying non-materialistic life around ideals. To ridicule them is by implication to ridicule ourselves. (To ridicule ourselves, on the other hand, is not far from our minds, as we mistake one turn of the road after another; we feel always on the brink of absurdity, that the whole enterprise of penetrating and ordering religion is surreal.)

We hear of physical therapy communities, where diet, exercise, and love build new souls, and of group therapy communities where, in one case, one learns to love oneself and, in another case, to give up selfish love of oneself to love others. We learn of astrological networks of believers who adjust their lives to the elaborated meaning of planetary motions and conjunctions.

There are communities and networks of *haute couture*, work, skills, fraternity, "rock and roll," sexual practices, diet, outer space communications, sports, and many other special areas that go far beyond occasional meetings and informational exchanges into the dense supernatural and ritual affairs of religious cults. They are voluntary. Participation may be brief and intense; it is for that period sacred, supernatural and ritualistic.

We begin to see an overall pattern of the people of a secular society; they live amidst many intense but sporadic religious episodes, where their minds are fully occupied in recapitulating birth, baptism, initiation, marriage, priesthood and death in brief compass, and in between these episodes, they float and paddle in a swirling world of secular symbols, legends, myths, and fictions. Are they happy? Have they found Truth and Morality? Once again, I would warn against a hasty denial. What is "happy"? Who is happy in this world? "Happy" may be a little thing, quite evasive, quite accidental and lucky, though subjectively grand in its effects.

As for "moral", that, too, may be the accident of a soul that is bumped and tossed about like flotsam, until finally jettisoned onto the shores of goodness.

CHAPTER TEN

ETHICS AND THE SUPERNATURAL

After a brief military campaign in the Falklands (Malvinas) Islands in 1982, memorial services for the dead of Great Britain and Argentina were held at the Cathedral of Canterbury, England. To some of the British, the idea of memorializing the Argentine dead was already irksome. Then going beyond ceremony, the Archbishop in his sermon deplored warfare, asserting that it proved the failure of a foreign policy. Whereupon he was verbally chastised by Prime Minister Thatcher and like-minded representatives of English jingoism for not having made it clear to the assembly that the British were righteous and victorious in the eyes of The God of the Established Church of England. Reasonably the one party might complain, of what use is the State Church if it does not support the State's wars? Just as reasonably, the Archbishop might say: Of what use is a religion if it cannot teach peace to politicians?

The peacemakers often go unblessed by the religions, too. Mirza Ahmad Sohrab, in his grand tome, *The Bible of Mankind,* compares the great world religions to the strings of a single harp each of which gives forth its own dominant note, while the harmonious blending of all produces a symphony of music. The dominant note of Hinduism is *the divine presence pervading nature;* of Buddhism, *remuneration;* of Zoroastrianism, *purity;* of Confucianism, *filial piety;* of Taoism, *the path to reason;* of Judaism, *righteousness;* of Christianity, *love;* of Islam, *submission,* and of the Bahai Cause, *universality,* "In their efforts to admit and confess all humanistic doctrines of religions, the Bahai have been frequently persecuted by god-fearing believers, and, even while the British were wrestling with Christian "love," the Bahai were being dispossessed and killed, allegedly for religious and statal treason , by Iranian Muslim practicing "submission" to Allah.

Secularists frequently pronounce religious slogans for lack of a substantial ethics of their own. Moral issues often intimidate secularists, too. There is a sacredness about them, a confusion, a threat, a secret, a god buried somewhere among them, a priest ready to pull one in like a fish if one takes the smallest bait.

There used to be a major area of study called "the moral sciences." It is defunct. In turn, every field of the natural sciences, social sciences and humanities has tried to extricate itself from moral responsibility and qualify for the name of science. Even practical schools of business, medicine, dentistry, law, agriculture, engineering, architecture, nursing, social welfare, etc., claim to provide an objective education; they have achieved the logically impossible feat of inculcating in their students an abundance of the best ways of doing things, while pretending not to consider good from bad, right from wrong.

We know this to be nonsense. All applied science most exhibit preferences for lines of conduct. Scientific method is itself a moral system. And just think of the vast proportion of alumni of schools who confess, with a quaver in their voices, to all that they know and owe to their alma mater. Somebody is teaching somebody something in the way of morals! What is happening?

Is this hypocrisy? Are the schools and students, the society and its people, claiming one thing and practicing another? Yes. They are using a technique that places upon an unreachable, untouchable level certain problems such as god, religion, and the supernatural, along with the associated problem of the ultimate sources of morality and their justification; they take up all other problems as only of instrumental importance, as problems of means, not ends, as problems whose solutions can be taught to burghers, brigands, and beggars alike.

Whereupon a society becomes secular, segmentalized and instrumental (hence exploitative) in its behavior as well as its morals. From many a segment are cast many grappling hooks for the larger morality, some of which catch hold and from here and there spring the many varieties of religious practices characteristic of the secularized society.

Where there is not a grappling for religion, there is often a contradictory pair of behaviors: the one a specialized nose-to-the-ground empiricism, the other a hopelessly dispersed attention. The former was discussed in the last chapter as an aspect of secularism and occurs again for treatment in the next; the latter requires a few more words here. Religion generally focuses attention onto a few, high-priority objects of value; secularism dissipates attention.

Attention is itself a value imposed on whatever is attended to. It is a preference for its object, selected out of all potential substitutes as objects of attention. Attention is instinctively determined in non-human creatures and modified by parental and group training in many species; the ambiant force impinging on the creature also helps to determine the objects of its attention. As with other creatures, man's attention in part is a valuing of the object, elementary, without training, without justification.

Very few persons will even admit that their valuational life is already half described when their attention spectrum is drawn up. But so it is, pathetic as it may be.

They would like to believe that attention is a real, natural, automatic experience, about which they promptly cogitate. This is Cartesian rationalism, for does he not offer as a first principle of his *Discourse on Method, cogito ergo sum,* "I sense that I perceive, therefore I am," and, further, "I perceive because I want, and therefore am."

So, straightaway with birth, we fix the infant, if he had a mind to wander, upon the right, proper, goods things - the nipple, the nurse, the movements of the nurse, her voice, his bowels moving, his eyes lightening, his muscles flexing, all following after the not so good things - his wonderment at himself, a loss of his boundaries, a panicky feeling of loss of his warm pool, stunned dissolution exposed into infinite space.

Suppose his family to be church-goers. He is habituated to church as soon as he can be counted upon to be quiet most of the time there. Time passes, and one day, when he hears, "We are getting ready for church," he displays a mind of his own. "Why?" "Because..." "Because of what?" "Because it's Sunday." "Why do we go to church on Sunday?" "To worship God." And so on. It is almost entirely a morality of means, that carries him from one step to the next, not "really explaining."

Sometimes this begins, or he is catechized, even if he asks no questions. "Why should I worship God?" "God gives us our blessings in life." "Like ice-cream?" "Yes." And like your mother, and father, and a bed to sleep in, and food to eat. To train him properly, the trainer is usually clever enough to number only things which the trainee likes. But there is small pay-off for the trainer unless he slips into the list of blessings things that he, the trainer likes. So they go to church to assure the blessings that each wants. They already have different religions, in a sense.

Still later on, the child has a habit of church-going, as a result of which, his authorities are happy to observe, he feels better with himself, when he attends, and guilty if he misses church. He knows people there, and may even enjoy an occasional service. Unfortunately for his educators, he now changes, we presume. He is bored and fidgety in church; people scowl at him. He does not get the blessings he especially wants. He is drawn to television, and wants to play baseball with the kids who do not go to church. Here are better rewards in his mind; though he has no doubt of God, God's command to "Worship Me in My House," does not get to him forcefully enough. He begins an argument with his educators that will go on for years.

What can be said of morality in this simple story? There is a great deal of moral training and moral response. The church and its religion are part of, and will always be part of the child's life. Unless he undergoes heavy secularization, he will possess hundreds of ethical views that are connected directly and indirectly with his religion. Almost none of them has come about through autonomous action, reasonable analysis, a survey of cases. The morals collect upon him like fuzz upon a rubbed glass rod.

I am saying merely what dozens of writers have said before me. With regard to practically all those who have practiced religion throughout history and today, the whole of religion may be regarded as a generally effective machine to structure a collection of behaviors and bring about their enforcement. The key to the ramshackle edifice is the reduction of cosmic, existential self-fear.

For all that religion has dominated the human world from its beginnings, its ethical results have been paltry. The one thing that is supposed to justify religion is precisely the thing that religion does worst, making the human a satisfactory ethical creature.

But it must be said that religion has forever assumed the most difficult of all tasks: supplying human existence with an objective morality. The problem is multiplex: how to deal with oneself, one's inner relations; how to deal with others; how to treat with the animate and inanimate world of nature. In the end, one is supposed to be able to say "ought" confidently, to live according to the same "ought," and to be happy. In all of this, one's morality ought to be consonant with the real world and its operating principles, science, that is. Hence, morality is the governance of behavior by rules for preferring and achieving certain human and natural relations and states of being.

Unfortunately the simplest, most general rules crack under the stress of psychology and anthropology. "Don't drive while drunk" is a reasonable rule. It should readily illustrate what Emmanuel Kant meant when he propounded his famous dictum: "Act only on that maxim through which you can at the same time will that it should become a universal law."

Yet Kant's rule, though it might work to his personal satisfaction, might bring about continual disasters if it were allowed to justify others, such as many suicidal and dying persons who would be pleased to have the whole world die with them. Even the drunk may a) deny that he cannot drive safely, b) suggest that everyone should enjoy a drunken drive from time to time, or c) suggest that drunken driving is a good way to play the necessary game of half-wishing self-destruction. If he does not express such ideas, it may be because he realizes that the police make no distinction between common drunks and drunk philosophers. But now we speak of authority, not Kantian rationalism.

If we ask what functions are performed by an ethical judgment, we get a more lively sense of this feeling. Feeling ethical, one praises or reprimands, one rewards and punishes another. This sometimes changes the behavior of the targets of such feelings in the direction desired by the moralist. More broadly, then, one exhibits a preference in order to arouse enthusiasm or indignation, to rally support. One raises an ethical feeling in order to determine a policy, and to get on with affairs in an orderly organized way. None of this would be done without our or someone's expression of value.

Subjectively, too, the very power to make an ethical judgment is a satisfaction in itself, which often is sufficient unto itself, regardless of consequences. To express one's feelings is in fact synonymous with giving vent to ethical judgments.

Alongside all of these functions is the one which religions stress but which very few people feel regularly, that is, to carry out the will of the gods or of the supernatural or fate or nature, because an ordinary resort to this function floods the sluiceways of personal and collective action; it is usually blocked very early in its manifestation. However, it can be the most powerful of all functions of ethical judgments, as we see in the Crusades, the Islamic conquests, or nowadays the rule over Iran by Khomeini.

We can agree. These are the functions of words. Man is irretrievably consigned to a life crowded with them. Morals are now a heap of functions as well as forces.

Thousands of unsuccessful moral philosophers attest to the frustrations abounding in the pursuit of morals. Voyaging to the Moon is less difficult than the problems of morally justifying the effort involved in the accomplishment. Nonetheless, all humans behave morally and always have. By moral behaviour, we mean acting one way rather than another because, among other reasons, one feels that it is right and good, and that not acting that way would be wrong and bad. This "feeling" is a "real" thing, physiologically compelling, with physical disturbance and mental states called frustration, indignation, anger, humiliation, and anxiety if the moral act is not performed and euphoria, satisfaction, and physical and mental relaxation if it is performed.

The easiest way to "solve" the moral question is to deny it, that is, to assert that people feel moral or immoral, right or wrong, in consequence of a heap of experience, commands, forces, and natural traits. There would be found in this heap no specific independent moral quality. Morality then is no more than what is in the definition above, "among other reasons."

The only fault that I can find with this idea is that I do not like the way people behave, and I feel that I am not alone in this regard, so I wish to change people. But how do I extricate a moral principle from the heap? Why should anyone else care what I like or what I do not like, unless I had power to force compliance with my morals and they would do well to obey my rules, or else - "lest you die ..." as Yahweh might say.

So I must search for "justification" of my morality (call it M). What is meant by justification?

1) What so appeals to those I wish to change (adopt my preference) that they change a) their attitude b) behaviour c) both. That is, I manipulate them. Nothing here can be considered the satisfying "justification" which I seek. I have, after

all, used completely knowable means to warp their wills and minds (" applied social science").

The forms of manipulation include: a) force; b) bribes; c) persuasion by symbols and propaganda, by example, by citing god, priests, scriptures; d) proof of advantages they derive *for* and *by* themselves (" 'x' or 'y' is good for you"). They will feel better, look better, etc.; e) 'logical' proof (" If you want 'X' do 'M'").

But in all of this (M) remains unjustified (except the *word of God,* but which they dispute, hence, is unjustified); that is, I have no right to inflict (M), that is, to change others.

2) So I examine myself. How does it happen that I a) do not like their behavior (M), b) want to change it (M) and I find many causes (reasons) for a) and many causes for b) which boil down to material benefits, property, convenience, and control. All of these are without validity so I must go on. I also feel embarrassment, guilt at *their* behavior.

3) Why am I guilty when *they* behave so.
   a. Identification: I feel that I am part of them and hence suffer their effects.
   b. Projection: I feel that their motives are my own.
   c. Self-punishment: I feel guilt *for* them.
For all of this, I change them.
But why do I feel guilt?
   a) Because I am trained to feel guilt.
   b) Because I want to behave like them or did once and was punished or harmed.
   c) Because of experience (e. g. "I let my younger brother behave so, and look at him now!")
So none of these justify either!

4) I listen to *My god,* and don't let them interpret *god* their way, and get support to suppress them.
But now my insight (still active) tells me I may be wrong *re* god. Is there any other means of justification?

5) Can I now say, "What I want is what I want, and it is, at least,

'good' in that if I get it, I satisfy whatever it is that makes me want it."

Now what is it that I am satisfying?

> a) A psycho-physiological process of which there are several, *viz.:* damping of fear, extension of control (over self, over others), displacement of affect, identification, obsession (repetition), ambivalence;
>
> b) possessing one or more of, more wealth (things); affection; power; well-being (safety, health, strength); respect; skill (knowledge).

Thus everything said of 1) to 4) beforehand may in fact be the superstructure of 5) here.

6) The only way I can budge from this position of 5) which has established my *Basic Morality* is *by changing myself* so that another different or an altered want takes the place of (M). But, if M_2 is substituted for M_1 (no matter how little time or how long it takes) then I am changed and have *a different morality*.

7) What can cause this different morality (M_2)?
a) Failure by resistance; b) accident; c) internal change (metabolism goes down, illness, different glandular flow, etc.)

8) Then I repeat M_2 with respect to the group of people whose actions I did not like before and go through 1) to 7) again.

9) Now is M_2 better than M_1 and will M_3 be better than M_2... M^n? How would one know?

10) Suppose M^x has these subsequences or consequences? It is significantly easier to run through the process. Further, no change occurs when it is achieved in me, i. e.

$$M^x = M^n, \text{ the final value of morality.}$$

11) Therefore, I settle upon M^x and practice M^x and all closely analogous $M^x_{a...n}$. This becomes in effect my moral system in regards to the class of behaviors we are discussing.

12) We note:
   a) M^x is mine, but also others' moral system because we are effectively transacting within its rules!
   b) The system is both *egoistic* and species-*racial* (social). It works. It can be mythicized, religified, philosophized.

In the sequence of events, 1) to 12), it will be noticed that all processes are explained in natural terms, as instances of well-known and common psychological and social dynamics. The supernatural is involved on the level of such fictions, concepts, perceptions, and illusions as are usually encountered in human psychic and social transactions.

Moral demands, moral behavior, and moral struggle are occurring. Ethical resolutions and principles are evolving. But it is all happening without resort to a moral source existing and coming from beyond the act and process themselves.

Let us consider the choices of a typical person, Abel. We assume that he makes an average of 140 choices a day, and therefore roughly 50,000 in a year. They range in significance, for example, from deciding whether to brush one's teeth quickly or thoroughly, to whether or not to begin setting aside $3,000 a year towards the college education of a child. If it is argued that brushing teeth is hardly a moral or ethical issue, one can either argue in rebuttal or simply raise the threshold of a moral question by some criteria of significance that excludes brushing the teeth.

Where this latter point would commence is not easy to define. Perhaps it should be an issue which, whatever its subject, involves conscience, that is, a slight or larger factor of anxiety and guilt pursuant to an uncertain decision (if it were to be uncertain). Since we are being so speculative, we can presume to estimate also that 10% of the decisions will have such a guilt factor, giving a total number of about 4,000 moral decisions per year, or about 13 per day.

Thus, one would count as containing the guilt factor: a choice of watching a television entertainment or doing school homework; drinking a second glass of whiskey or not; deciding how much money to put in the church collection box; whether or not to eat a gourmet garlic sauce before going on a blind date; slapping a child; etc. We shall not attempt a fine mathematical analysis of our typical citizen, Abel, but merely assign him categories and percentages, basing the categories on the kinds of mentation occurring as the decision is made. (The classification is obviously slap-dash.)

TYPES OF MORAL MENTATION BY HYPOTHETICAL TYPICAL CITIZEN (On Annual Basis)

A.	Practically automatic	40%	2,000
B.	Conscious, sloganized	20%	1,000
C.	Rationalized gibberish	15%	800
D.	Carefully calculated	1%	50
E.	Passionate, intuitive	5%	250
F.	Troubled by aware internal conflicts	5%	250
G.	Troubled by aware social conflict	6%	300
H.	Flights of fancy, fantasy, solipsism	7%	350
-	-	100%	5,000

Thus, imagining one certain day in his life, Abel might make the following ethical choices:

Moral Action	Type of Mentation Involved
Withholding a child's allowance	F
Giving a seat to an elderly lady on the bus	A
Overcharging a tiresome client	E
Working a little overtime on his job	A
Fantasyzing adultery with an attractive woman	H
Buying a lottery ticket	A
Absorbing news of a friend's death	C
Angered by a newspaper article on crime	A
Explaining his preference for a politician	B
Commenting on an office quarrel	F
Wondering whether to bring home a cake	B
Deciding to be "sick" and not work one day	D
Signing a negative report on an employee	G

It happens, we say, that each of these decisions gave Abel a moral twinge; the other 117 moral choices did not. Other people will have different numbers, types, and intensities of moral action in a day's time. If one reads James Joyce's *Ulysses,* a fictional masterpiece on a day in the life of Leopold Bloom in Dublin, Ireland, taking up some hundreds of pages of print, we realize that we are probably greatly underestimating the profusion of ethical choices in a 24 hour period.

Yet I have no idea of the range, average, or typical kinds of moral actions in a day's time. People are called by those who know them "conscientious," "unconcerned," "busy-body," etc., words that must refer to the extent and types of their moral behavior, but the appropriate sample survey with what happens in moral discourse of the self with itself and others has very little resemblance to the kinds of problems analyzed by philosophers and imagined by most preachers and teachers. Bloom, the character, had, I guess, an unusually active mind and more conflicts to resolve by the nature of his background, romantic wife, advertising work, avidity for many things in life, and continuous movement about the city.

Still, we have enough of exemplary material and a frame of reference to allow suggesting several points about moral mentation and action. The average life presents a great abundance of moral choices. The form of mentation employed before, after, and in the course of acting morally is largely absurd. Only a small portion of it is related to science or theory except indirectly. Only a tiny percentage of a modernized population spends much moral energy on the divine, or on methodical calculation (unless it is one's paid job to do so).

In *Civilization and Its Discontents* Sigmund Freud points out the commonly known problem of ethics:

> that ill-luck - that is, external frustration - so greatly enhances the power of the conscience in the super-ego. As long as things go well with a man, his conscience is lenient and lets the ego do all sorts of things; but when misfortune befalls him, he searches his soul, acknowledges his sinfulness, heightens the demands of his conscience, imposes abstinences on himself and punishes himself with penances. Whole peoples have behaved in this way, and still do.

He calls this an "original infantile state of conscience."

> Fate is regarded as a substitute for the parental agency. If a man is unfortunate, it means that he is no longer loved by this highest power; and, threatened by such a loss of love, he once more bows to the parental

representative in his super-ego - a representation whom, in his days of good fortune, he was ready to neglect.

Fate is looked upon as an expression of Divine Will. Fatalism is very strong in early religions and ethics. Why? The authorities and experts say: because primitive man was at the mercy of savage natural forces. Still, if man were to be of the same *ideological cast* today, he would also be fatalistic because obviously, when one think of it, very little *real* control has been exercised over the immense and infinite area of difficulties besetting us. Rather, the change of attitude has come about as a result of changed ideology, *Weltanschauung*, and this has changed because of a fairly long calm condition of the Earth and the skies, and the development of a progressive, free-will, uniformitarian (self-contradictory) philosophy. Perhaps the distinction between traditional sacral and modern secular man is that the former has not forgotten his primeval scenarios, whereas the latter has suppressed them very deeply and become overtly pragmatic.

John C. Caldwell wrote a memorandum, not formally published, on the Sahelian Drought of the 1970's. We take leave to quote him lengthily:

Fatalism

Fatalism is an unsuitable term because it can be used in two ways: to mean the rational acceptance by those living in a traditional society that they have little control over the forces affecting their lives; and to mean such a reluctance to attempt any control that they are more battered by such forces than need be the case.

The acceptance of the blows of fate is often so great in traditional society that it is difficult to measure the personal impact of disaster or even to discuss it properly. Often technical aiders give up the attempt and go to talk to other technical aiders who seem to speak the same language, and thereby sustain the conventional wisdom and often lose all chance of adding to worthwhile knowledge about the situation. Sometimes they wonder if they have been entirely misled about the reality of the position. In one of the few honest reports ever written on this question, a transport expert working intimately with the truck drivers bringing food relief in the recent Sahelian drought and having substantial contact with the rural population reported that at first none of the local population seemed ever to have heard of the drought; later he concluded that they felt it deeply and were taking rational steps to minimize the hurt in ways they had known all their lives... In Yelwa, northwest Nigeria, it was reported that, "The Emir of Yauri and the Divisional Officer, head of the Local Administration, held that drought did not occur in Yelwa and that no problem with shortage of rains was extant". Even the farmers talked of locusts, weeds and lack of good lands as much as drought.

There are many reasons for this kind of reaction. One is that the matter is irrelevant to the outsiders, whose lives are demonstrably not affected by the climatic conditions. Another is a belief, held also by the outsiders, that nothing can be done to alter the weather. Actually this view is usually more rational still -- a feeling that the bad years are as much part of the totality of what must be experienced as the good years and that the lot of man is to bend with each wind. Such attitudes are embedded deep in the culture; they find religious expression and are reinforced by religion. In much of the savannah and desert of Africa, people take drought to be a necessary divine warning that religious and moral standards are slipping and that a revival is due. Drought provides assurance that Providence is paying attention and is still concerned. It indicates a need for religious leaders to intercede with God. If the drought is long and severe, resort will also be made to age-old methods, long predating Islam, for encouraging rain... From the Western Sahel to Somalia drought and religious observations are deeply linked.. In profane literature and oral tradition references, the need for water [is] equally pervasive. In these circumstances it is not surprising that the common man is somewhat apprehensive about recalling the last drought or predicting the next one. The Yelwa survey reported that, although there was clear agreement about the nature and seriousness of drought, there was complete disagreement in the farmers' responses as to when the last one occurred and three-quarters did not wish to encourage bad luck (or to trespass into the domain of Allah) by suggesting that one would ever again occur...

Not only is the origin of drought either divine or in any case not to be influenced by Man, but so is death -- a proposition that is still true over most of the Sahel most of the time. Western doctors working in the drought refugee camps were disturbed when the mothers of dying children seemed to be more concerned about obtaining cloth to serve as shrouds for their dead or dying babies than they appeared to be about the fact of death itself. Their reaction were partly explained by the fact that the babies had symptoms which have always presaged death in the savannah. Part, too, was the religious conviction that the babies were being called away and had been destined at this time to leave the world (the Fulani express it as the child wanting to go.) These are not societies in which determined efforts are likely to be made to counter the condition of an apparently dying child or indeed to prevent the births of children. Urbanization and other types of economic modernization ultimately lower child mortality both by providing greater health services and by convincing people that one can and should intercede with the forces that determine children's sickness and death.

We see how sacral man confronts secular problems and converts them into forms amenable to sacred solutions.

The thousands of cultures existing in historical time and space have given us a fair sample of the ideal and practical ethical capabilities of religion. The experience on the whole has been unimpressive to one looking for a happy human way of life. The more one trusts to religion, it seems, the less good one can obtain from science and politics. On the other hand, science in itself (that is, science which is entirely positive and empirical) is quite helpless to address the moral perplexities of man.

Politics, moreover, has, if anything, a poorer record than religion, speaking now of politics as a secular approach to human issues; for politics tends by itself to depend upon sheer physical force to order a population, and systematic violence is hardly an improvement upon whatever chicanery and delusions historical religions employ to rule a people. Would one have preferred to be governed by the barons or by the monks of the European Middle Ages, by the warlords or by the Shinto and Buddhist priests of Old China, by the shaman or by the priest, by Aaron or by Joshua? And, today in America, if the lawyers, lobbyists, and military contractors were replaced in the ruling circles and representative assemblies of the country by ministers, priests, and the religiously devout, would the country be better governed, its people more peaceable, mentally healthy, and prosperous? Would one prefer to be governed by the Ayatollah Khomeini or by the Shah of Iran?

The questions are difficult, enormously complicated, and perhaps biased. Still they are worth considering if only as a means of suggesting that ethical progress in a society is not to be identified with its secularization. The key to good governance is an ethical system beyond facile contrivance. Neither religion nor secularism, as such, promises success.

Even though it may be true that our morals come in a tangled concatenation, the human could scarcely accept the fact. One whose overriding aim is self-control and control over the world will refuse to recognize in a garbage pile his towering morality. This in itself would seem to prove him a moral failure - shifty, gutless, inconsistent, contradictory (all that he really is, someone might comment). He feels that there must be an absolute, pure source of right conduct somewhere, and is all too ready to find and proclaim one, even an impostor.

Yet occasionally the human becomes ashamed of living a lie and hates himself and hates his religion and gods for having created his dependency upon delusions. He admires the "honesty" of the bear, the trout, the dog; they are not of two minds and forked tongue. Why cannot his morality be so straightforward?

Blame part of it upon his obsession with history, his compulsion to repeat his worst experiences. He demands that his morality today be that of five thousand years ago. He demands that it be of the highest order: we know what that means; it must come from Heaven. Further he demands that all people share in an ecumenical morality. The logical and sociological impossibility of both demands will not deter him. He is implacable. He will not pluck his morals from a garbage heap.

What can the scientist counsel? Try as they might, the anatomist and physiologist cannot separate a pig and a man far enough for comfort. The biologist, try as he may, cannot worship an arrangement derangeable by an unseen particle, and a lucky hit out of hundreds of millions of spermatozoa. Try if he would, the anthropologist could not work up an agitation over adulterous intercourse and let the commandment be written down by the hand of a god. Nor can the geologist see in an awful blasted out crater more than a crashing meteoroid. Nor the astronomer see more than a vast number of worlds in just that, a vast number of worlds: it seems that the gods, too, have a compulsion to repeat. No, the scientists cannot appease their consciences and man's sacrality with any consistency.

Besides providing people with morality, it is said, religion puts them directly in touch with the supernatural realm. For the mass of people this is untrue, just as it is that their religion gives them some special ethical competence. A few practitioners must enjoy the facilities for communion with the spiritual universe which churches and temples provide. The mass media (motion pictures especially) and drugs, as T. Leary has eloquently argued along with others, and, too, many gurus, seances, and non-church rites provide this type of communion.

The supernatural is hard to distinguish from political illusions and fictions. To the practitioners of scientific method, a devotee of astrology and a political fascist share several features. Both analyze the present state of world and personal affairs, and gain confidence and make predictions on the basis of their beliefs. Knowing that a person is an astrologist or, on the other hand, a fascist, enables the social psychologist to assert and predict with high probability that each will possess certain attitudes. The fascist believes in his leader as the possessor of semi- divine qualities, a superman. He has a warped conception of history and the future (according to our scientists). The astrologist believes his astrologer has access to supernatural knowledge; he, too, has a warped conception of the path of history and the future. Both types are paranoiac in believing that a great deal of what is really happening in the world is concealed by the establishment or conspiratorial powers.

The far departure from reality in both cases may have little to do with their success in life. General knowledge and matter-of-factness are only loosely connected with achievement in society. The belief of both the astrologist and the fascist in the supernatural lends each a confidence denied to less convinced persons; self-confidence is in many life situations more of an asset than knowledge of the situation. Whereas the ordinary human is only schizotypical, these two tend more towards the schizophrenic.

We seem to be at an impasse, owing to my downgrading of the creative moral and spiritual functions of historical religion. Supernaturalism appears to be all manner of anti-scientific folly. Morality exists concerning countless particulars in human activities, even while neither religion nor secularism can justify its source, hence their application.

We see no easy solution, perhaps none at all. Later on, we may offer some grounds to justify a "relatively absolute" morality, meaning by this verbal barbarism some unchanging moral propositions that are themselves changing. If one might conceive of a religion that is an integrated whole, accommodates change easily, and that does not fundamentally and continuously violate the controls and benefits supplied by science, then this religion may not only be superior but also popular.

Does this mean that morality is human and mundane, part of an endless process going on in millions of transactions every day everywhere? Yes. Does it mean that the supernatural, the divine, the gods are not the source of morality, that ethics exists without religion? Yes. Does it mean that mankind is morally *sui generis* and autonomous? Yes.

Does it mean that humans are "immoral" and "wicked," with no means of setting ethical standards? No. Does it mean that the supernatural, all that is divine and sacred, has no effect upon ethical behavior? No.

The supernatural, as non-knowledge, is knowledge of a sort. Those who transact or seek to transact with the supernatural in order to think upon the divine, engage in an ideational relation with the divine, and are affected by the knowledge which we possess of the divine. They will behave differently than those who deny the supernatural and avoid it.

Religion, to put it in commonplace language, can make people better. It should be the "right" kind of religion, and, of course, this would be the form we are here advocating: self-aware, open, relativistic, non-historical, connected with the sciences of natural and socio-psychological processes, non-anthropomorphic morphologically, anthropomorphic structurally. Let us see what science is doing that is religiously relevant and can be adapted to religion.

CHAPTER ELEVEN

RELIGIOUS ELEMENTS IN SCIENCE

Out of religion came politics and then science, each reacting upon the others while going its own way. Science is a set of interests that is religiously, socio-politically, and autonomously determined. Science struggles to conform to a scientific method in whatever it does. The struggle lends it its distinction, providing it with its social character. Without the method, it is useless to speak of science. The method is applied to whatsoever extension of the senses is of interest and controls such extension; both operations sometimes fail but also often succeed in our day.

A scientific procedure typically puts forth a hypothesis about what is measurably expected to occur under certain conditions, and, by finding or producing the conditions, finds or produces the event. Wherever conditions permit, these are produced under controls; wherever they occur naturally, they are overseen as strictly as possible. No place is allowed in theory for supernatural conditions or supernatural effects, that is, for the intervention of factors that are undefinable in material terms, or of an external ungovernable will.

As Alexander Hamilton quipped, when Benjamin Franklin suggested prayer at an impasse while composing the American Constitution in 1787, we should not call upon the help of a foreign power. Hamilton, intending for politics what Franklin had already practiced in electrical experiments, had in mind a republic whose behavior might be predictable when certain regular operating conditions were established by its structure.

The incident reminds us that science includes social as well as natural science. Humans are a material factor in the one, if not in the other; they are a contaminating factor in both. The human factor has so continually disturbed the scientific method in its application to natural phenomena that, in a sense, all science becomes social science, especially as the material conditions of study become more difficult and less amenable to continuous ordinary sense observation. We cannot go here into the progressive discoveries of the intervention of anthropo-sociology and especially psychology in the workings of natural science, citing the works of P. W. Bridgman and others, but we can, without fear of rebuttal, warn of the inevitable effects upon experimenters and researchers of their psychological as well as physical presence amidst the supposedly materially and logically observer-proof conditions of scientific work.

Already, then we have to be on the alert, in all that passes as science-applying-scientific-method, so as to detect the interest that inspires the work and to discern the sometimes exceedingly subtle intervention of the mind in the process of discovery, proof, and disproof. The "interest" in a scientific task may range from the most banal, obvious, and limited (e. g. to polish better a lens so as to see stars more clearly; to adjust the angle of a spade to bite the ground with less energy input) to the general and ideological, that is, unconscious (e. g. to validate evolution by setting up hypotheses implying or excluding neo-darwinian evolution; to calculate pre-historical sky charts by retrocalculating or presumptively modifying present motions of the Earth and Solar system).

The aggregation of "outside" interests creates a continual uneasiness in scientific work; like barnacles on a fine yacht, it keeps science from being "clean;" but the barnacles are part of life at sea: no barnacles, no sailing. We may sympathize with scientists who call up their psychic mechanisms of unconscious denial by indignation at the idea that they may be skirting the supernatural, or, worse, serving the supernatural, or by backing up into ever narrow slips of material phenomena where it is hoped that none can say that anything but sense data are implicated in their work. The search for a body of pure science, however, like the search for the Golden Fleece, eventuates in taking aboard a witch with the long-sought prize, and Jason and his Argonauts must move on evermore in unresting adventure.

The main theories of astronomy are as remote from experience as to be spooky. Astronomers walk on a tightrope between science and religion, depending upon a few principles that are empirically formulated to keep the field aloft as a science. The most that astronomers can say empirically is that much of the universe, including fortunately most of the solar system, exhibits some large uniformities of behavior. As soon as they retroject or project by thousands of years they become vulnerable, that is, unbelievable.

The theories include largely a set of Newtonian laws that are fading fast and may soon be abrogated, and which serve to fire projectiles from the Earth in the direction of objects in space, such that, by deft *ad hoc* maneuvering, arrive on target. Otherwise, they boast Laplace's mathematical explanations, which Laplace himself declared to be dependent upon uniformitarian premises. Then there occur various ways of measuring brilliance, heat, distance, chemistry, speed, and chronology of heavenly bodies, which are hopeful speculations, thanklessly spared from all but an iota of factual proof, leaning upon one another for support but also begging each other's question.

So great, however is faith in the one "law of falling bodies" that all else passes as science simply because, as I said, the proof of science is the scientific method, and all of astronomy, by this time, has become couched in scientific form. That some of the more famous astronomers and related scientists of these decades - Urey, Hoyle, Wickramasinghe, Crick, T. Gold, and Sagan, to name only several, have toyed with bizarre theories impermissible to laymen, acknowledges the essential fragility and defensive posture of the field. Nowadays an astronomer, provided that he has an appropriate university degree, can profess the Doppler Effect, Bode's Law, intelligence in other worlds, the "Big Bang", the Laplace theorems, empty space, straight lines, exact solar time and motions, and a dozen other mostly conventional concepts. Whatever the mix, it is apparently unsystematic, unreliable, ad hoc, and temporary. If scientists lay claim to authority on grounds that such a mix is true and fully representative of reality, they can deny a "union card" to whoever disturbs the mix. If, however, they place claims of authority in the procedures of scientific method, then they must give a respectful hearing to any educated person who seeks to establish an identity for Plato's "divine animal" in the universe or to prove empirically any number of such hypotheses.

The same kind of reasoning can be directed at biology and geology. Basic conventional theories in both of these areas of study are weak and straining at the point of collapse into disintegration, if not supernaturalism. No more than physics can define energy other than by fiction, operations and hypothesis, can biology define life. Fringe life forms are several, with subatomic behavior, crystals, and viruses providing initial confusion, and sending practitioners to more comfortable empirical fields to work. Ethology is rampant in the fields distinguishing among animals. Evolutionary theory is a shambles; "natural selection" is invoked as often as God in the Bible, but it is an embarrassment to do so.

The Earth Sciences, like the other fields, are making many advances to which the name "revolutionary" is increasingly applied with some pride. Yet two of their greatest operational concepts - that of time and that of uniformitarian change - are in peril. They invest much hope in radiochronometry to preserve long time spans and therefore smooth out curves of change, but, as I have explained elsewhere, radiochronometry is based upon radioactivity which is affected by the kind of history that it claims to prove; that is, catastrophe destroys time even while time pretends to disprove catastrophe.

Psychology and anthropology include so many variations of methodology that discerning the supernatural in them is not difficult; only the naive can persistently believe that variant methods are independent of moral perspectives, simply grasping the struggling corpus by a toe instead of its nose. Every psychological or anthropological "school" is a supernatural sect, whether it seeks to confront the supernatural or turn its back to it.

But, although moral and supernatural, science in itself is not capable of justifying human action; it cannot even justify its own. The myth that it can, which was exposed as soon as science was mature enough to bear the truth, lives on like any other supernatural belief, lending motivation, inflaming passions, claiming moral credits, inspiring lives, and narrowing thought and options. Probably, too, many scientific secularists labor in the hope that something marvellous and morally convincing will grow out of their work, as penicillin emerged serendipitously from a mould.

Willy-nilly all sciences, in their healthy vigor, are wrestling with the supernatural and contributing to its expansion thereby. In this sense, all sciences are addressing the foundations of religion and theology. The more scientific work that is performed, the more areas of uncontrollability and contradiction come upon the stage. Science itself is the biggest factory of the supernatural. It tears holes in the fabrics extending reality. It works all the while surrounded by amateurs of the supernatural and theologians, pelted by derision. Perhaps one might forecast the most esteemed and influential religion of the future by locating the contemporary cult that is closest to the anomalies and radical new interests of science.

Theology can be a science, whether it be formulated as pure or as applied science. As the latter, it can be called religious science, or, simply, religion, just as certain departments of political science in American universities call themselves departments of politics (New York University) or departments of government (Harvard University), both of these terms meaning applied political science. A proposition (hypothesis) in theology might then read: "All cultures denominate historical gods."

We suppose that this proposition, empirically tested, may eventuate with exceptions, such as the Buddhists or the Union of Soviet Socialist Republics and possibly several other totalitarian socialist regimes. Then, if we wish, we may restate the proposition, as some have, to include "pseudo-gods," saying that "a god includes a figure with 3,4...n attributes of which at least 'x' have to be present to permit the designation 'god' to be used." Hence certain cultures have figures such as Lenin or Mao Tse Tung who possess at least 'x' attributes, while others have celestial figures that border upon gods such as Region 'A' in China where "Heaven" (Ti'en) is accorded at least 'x' traits of a god, and still others elevate masters and gurus to the stature of Muhammad.

We perceive that the pure proposition is heading in a certain direction and that by the manipulation of the definition of the term "god," certain areas of empirical research are opened up, and, furthermore, that some hidden intent may even be present, such as to demonstrate the ineradicability of the worship of gods.

A related proposition in applied theology or religion can continue to illustrate the nature of theology and at the same time show how applied propositions formulate matters often more transparently, from the viewpoint of ideological research. Thus, one says: "To disestablish gods of traits 'a.... n' including 'g' and 'h' it is necessary to establish a totalitarian regime with semi-divine figures of traits 'a... n' less 'g' and 'h'."

So elementary an introduction will hardly persuade anyone of the profundity and possibilities of theology as a science. The reader may be justifiably impatient to hear what theology can do with propositions of the supernatural. He may be wanting to know whether the supernatural exists, for example, and how the science of theology proves this.

One ought not be evasive; nevertheless, it must be pointed out, in anticipation of the answer to this question, that no science pretends to answer impossible questions, even though these may be scientifically formulated and studied. Medicine has few researchers (perhaps one-ten thousandth of its energies?) given over to the long-term prolongation of human life, although this may be a strong interest of the public. Nor are many astrophysicists preoccupied with voyages of a duration greater than a few seconds of a light-year. Nor are many political scientists or psychologists devoted to the attainment of utopias. That is, one can conceive of a flourishing science of theology that concerns itself hardly at all with proving hypotheses on the existence of the supernatural (and, indeed, may flourish for that very reason, just as chemistry flourished only after it stopped seeking for an Elixir of Life and to transmute lead into gold).

So warned, we can put forward a proposition that deals with the central interest that many people have in religion. One may hypothesize thus: "The spiritual, defined as any event contradicting existing laws of science relating to materiality, and probably non-reproducible by known scientific procedures does (or does not) exist." I see no objection to arguing that this statement is scientific. For instance, let us suppose that a person claims to achieve a certain vision, that no one else can see. (" No one" here means nobody in a large random sample of a population to which the visionary belongs.) Suppose an adept in drug-use demonstrates that 'X' percent of the population, to whom a certain drug is administered, claim the same vision as 'A. ' The vision is therefore proven to be possible, although not proven to deal with real objects. A scientific explanation of 'A' is not forthcoming, even though the state of 'A' is reproducible. Theology takes in consequence the position that the vision itself is actual, that 'A' and possibly some other rare persons are capable of it, and that many others can attain it upon taking the certain drug. Obviously we are not faced with a powerful proof of the existence of the supernatural.

But suppose that 'A' reports that this vision is of a vaguely defined human form who tells him "You shall see my power at Bunting Green Airport in 48 hours." Two days later a plane crashes at said airport. This has happened while a quarter of the large sample has been taking the drug and many of these had images predicting dire events at the same airport or some airport at roughly the same time. It would not require many cases of this sort to prove the validity of this type of supernaturalism (the type is very commonly asserted in legends, mythology, and religious documents, as, e. g., when Yahweh tells Moses to fetch the Elders on the Holy Mountain to be near The Lord and they come and do see the Lord. (Exodus *24*)

However, if one were a foundation grants officer he might give money to the "control group drug study" as described, but not in any expectation of a resulting by-product such as the air crash prediction. For he would be warned by practically every alert and informed person that cases such as this occur only insofar as visionary figures make predictions and that the predicted events practically never occur. If you cannot expect definite and defensible results from it, you should not grant funds to a project. Never mind the appeal that to prove god at work once in a million projects is enough.

Suppose yet another type of proposal comes before the foundation. This asserts that, "Totemism in religion functions to repress human creativity, while anthropomorphism in religion increases it." The applicant conjectures simply that if people imitate an animal, even in imaginary behaviors, they will not become very clever, whereas if they imitate an equally fictional superman, they will become more clever. "Imitation" is, of course, defined and measured operationally as part of religious totemism and anthropomorphism, as are the concepts "totemism," "anthropomorphism," and "creativity."

Whatever the results of such an inquiry, which is highly relevant both to anthropology, where pre-existing theories of the origins of totemism amount to over forty, and to theology, where, whether or not one believes in the well-nigh universal anthropomorphism, it is useful to know how it functions in the social structure, they are relevant to main lines of investigation in these fields and *a priori* must be useful.

Our imagined foundation is not likely to look so kindly, however, upon another proposal which crosses its threshold proposing to show that A) Moses' monotheism is anti-democratic and B) leads to politically harmful ideas of the supernatural among persons steeped in its learning. If government-financed and American, the foundation might decide that support for the program might be liable to court action on grounds that it violated the constitutional guarantee against abridgment of the freedom of religion, even though the argument might be advanced that the Constitution has the right to discover and protect itself against potential enemies.

A private scientific foundation would probably decide that the study would bring in no valid or useful results. The probable pro-Moses trustees would also determine that such a study is not scientific, even if the word "harmful" were replaced by several categories of consequences, empirically verifiable and undeniably relevant, such as "proneness to belief in charismatic authority," "totalitarian," "highly ethnocentric," and "highly aggressive and non-conciliatory."

Perhaps the term "anti-democratic" might escape similar close scrutiny, although quite vague and usually meaningless as employed; here again, the proponents of the research would no doubt advance empirical indicators, such as scoring high in attitude tests of tolerance, respect for discussion, consultation with others, compromise in decision-making, belief that opposing views may be right, and relative immunity from paranoia and hallucinations.

In sum, expertly espoused, the project could rebut all attacks against its scientificity, and certainly would transport scientific method into the core materials of theology. But it would be unlikely to win support. Generally speaking, scientific investigations have scarcely been employed in the field of theology proper. To the degree that theology in a given setting could be studied scientifically, it is deprived of the means, the intervening variable being indifference. This can be promptly and cheaply demonstrated by examining the articles in standard encyclopaedias having to do with the field and those who have worked in it. What is to be observed, creeping into the area from its fringes, are studies in anthropology, ethnology, sociology, political sociology, and psychology, few of which ever gain entry except through works such as Mircea Eliade's in the history of religion or works carrying a favorable attitude (from the standpoint of the market in ideas) such as Henri Bergson's and Teilhard de Chardin's or Hans Kung's.

A group of scholars working in the area with an approach termed "creation science" have developed their own audience and market. Their efforts to correlate natural history with sacred scripture qualify for the field of theology, too, and there is nothing un-scientific about quoting words attributed to Elohim or anyone else as a hypothesis for testing human or natural history. One would not refuse as the hypothesis for the study of, say, American politics (1965-80), or of history generally, a quotation attributed to an historian, Harold Acton, "All power tends to corrupt; absolute power tends to corrupt absolutely." One would however have to assure himself of the usual criteria: that "power," "absolute" and "corrupt" are operationally defined, and empirical indicators or measures provided for them.

When certain scholars determine to test the veracity of the Bible by quoting therefrom "God said to Noah... I will bring down a flood of waters upon the earth, to destroy all flesh in which is the breath of life from under heaven; everything that is on the earth shall die," and plan to adduce evidence from natural history of such a deluge, they are certainly proposing an ambitious project. And to qualify as scientists, they must clarify precisely, hypothetically, the extent of the destruction that is mentioned and its main instrument, a watery deluge, then validate by geological and ethnological evidence the occurrence of this particular flood (as distinct from a series of floods, etc.) And they would have to eschew any direct test of whether in fact the conversation took place between Elohim and Noah, because it is unverifiable. Most scientists would be logically compelled to accept a properly drafted study proposal of this type as belonging to the realm of scientific work.

Some scholars, gripped in the avoidance mechanism previously alluded to, would deny the relevance of any study whatsoever that would tend to confirm a scriptural statement. When one examines an encyclopaedia such as the *Britannica* which assigns millions of words to theological matters and many more millions to geology and ancient history, with only a dozen paragraphs treating the Deluge issue, whether as an issue or as a disputable event, and when one considers that the Deluge problem has agitated all generations of man everywhere since the beginning of history and before, one is inclined to ask, at least in this instance: "Who is the more biased against science: the creation scientists accepting scientific terms, or the editors of the *Encyclopedia Britannica* avoiding the subject unconsciously?"

Waiving the question, whose intent is obviously polemical, one may note once again how important is the matter of "interests" and the motives for such interests in science. The choice of subjects for hypothesis and study is obviously crucial in human culture and welfare, and yet has little to do with scientific method but much to do with the meaningfulness of science. And what is "meaning"? And who shall determine it?

"Meaning" is certainly among the most profound questions of philosophy and theology. "Why do we exist?" "What is our destiny?" If scientists choose to interest themselves, or are forced to occupy themselves with research on the advertising of commodities and with the perfection of weapons of destruction, to the extent say of ten thousand times the efforts put into the most meaningful questions of human existence, then they can hardly complain that the profound questions are overvalued.

One is led, therefore, to suggest that the supernatural is a proper and major concern for scientists, even if successes in the field come hard and require that they conduct humbling investigations of themselves. Perhaps a tithe of ten per cent of one's scientific energies and resources to theology is in order, and a similar tithe to the basic needs of humanity in regard to a basic minimum material subsistence, a basic possibility of gaining life experience through free movement and education, and a basically equal access to disinterested justice in all situations of conflicts of desire or interest. For, in this latter regard, scientific effort is also hugely biased against giving itself over to just those problems that render mankind incapable of an adequate material substratum of meaningfulness.

It is from the basic desire for new experience that the interest in the supernatural emerges. To stunt it, by allowing it a meaningless diet according to the scientific method, is a form of deliberate, if unconscious, deprivation, just as much as to stunt it by forcing it into obsessive narrow ritual which has nothing to do with scientific method.

Under such circumstances, it becomes ironical indeed to speak of "meaningless" propositions, as many modern logical positivist philosophers call considerations of the supernatural, for it is precisely against their "meaningless" reductionism that religious man is rebelling. "Words" are important in thought, but to carve them down into nothingness except as they have rigid and narrow denotations is but an unconscious method of assuring that the thought that occurs is to be equally rigid and narrow.

The kind of person who is then to be fashioned out of the raw material of *homo sapiens schizotypus* comes to depend upon only very limited mechanisms of fear-control, to wit, obsessed and catatonic behavior according to scientific rules, with a limited capacity for displacement of the selves of a person, a limited ability to identify the selves with the larger human and natural world, a severely suppressed ambivalence turning back upon the self, and a general lack of animation of the psyche. Surely this is not the intent of science, which only hopes to use words instrumentally and to solve otherwise impossible problems by a sure-fire method; but it does tend to be the effect of science when science exceeds its logical limits, demands to be "pure," and goes so far as to restrict its own method to areas guaranteed not to possess deep human meaning.

We can take up two attitudes in the face of the threat posed by many scientists to human development. One is that scientists are bound to fail in this method of coping with man's essential madness. "Just be patient; the movement will collapse from its inherent weaknesses," and indeed scientists do feel an overpowering weakness, and ensuing exasperation, when human cultures fail to embrace their interests and techniques or, worse, fashion crazy worlds of science-fiction to dwell in while waiting for science to solve all problems without the aid of politics or religion.

A second attitude, much to be preferred, is to encourage science in every way possible to examine itself and proceed to the examination of human nature, upon whose basic mechanisms science, politics, and religion must ultimately depend. What must this human being be fed to keep him creative and within bounds? The answer may be scientific theology. Bring together all that science is producing, half-consciously, in the way of theological findings and blend them into an integrated metaphysics, the whole of which addresses, not "mythical" or "rational" man, but the operative *homo sapiens schizotypus*.

I have examined human mental structure and operations in other works, so am permitted to relate here only the central relation of religion and science, and of this most clues are already familiar to the reader. Science emerges from the limited but most significant ability of the human mind to capture pragmatically, that is, to control, the connections between the person and an immense world of identifications and displacements. From his very beginnings, mankind has identified and sought to control the heavens and the gods, the mountains and oceans, the plants and animals. No other being on Earth is so ambitious; all others are confined to such rational activity as instinct requires for the purpose of survival and propagation.

The human mind, disordered by genesis and at birth, has the immense problem of extending pseudo-instinctive (that is, voluntary) controls over connections with existence that have very little to do with survival and propagation. The human, for instance, will sacrifice (both in the functional and symbolic senses) everything - food, family, sex, lesser powers, safety - in his efforts to command the skies.

Furthermore, besides the skies, there is many another realm of being that he is compelled by his mind to deal with, an infinite set of realms it seems, even though his mind, we must remember, is assisted by only moderately competent sensory organs, so that he is encumbered in his ingesting, questing, and adjusting.

So the need to order one's head requires that the cosmos be set in order, and it is natural for one to apply the pragmatic (scientific) techniques that substitute for instinct in the obtaining of both very close necessities and the most faraway necessities, and hence the elaboration of science out of immediate pragmatism occurs on both the intimate material level and the cosmic level.

Science is a human activity and therefore can be characterized as such, no less than religion is a human activity. It has a history, a sociology, a sub-culture, a psychology. It exhibits struggle, cooperation, ambition, failure, success, inducements - payoffs and penalties, a total range of material subjects to study, just as religion is subject of study, by the scientific method. It has religious and political aspects. It deals in authority, fictions, myths, claims, anomalies, rituals, and hypotheses, all of which are perilously reminiscent of religion and the supernatural. And, of course, to distinguish it especially from all other social activities, it is obsessed with the secular ritual of scientific method, and tends to extend the practice to all spheres of life.

The basic rite of scientific method is similar everywhere. But there come into being elaborations, embellishments, and variations of the basic rite. Some scientists like to think of the changes in naming, conceptualization, procedures, research interests, and so on as "progress" or at least "different ways of looking at the same thing." Other scientists know that they are in the grip of fashion and fads, whether in astronomy or geology, psychology or sociology. Magic, cultism, and other overtones, usually sounded and noticed in religious practice, can be heard in any science.

Every science must have a supernatural auxiliary. I would call it a suprascience, if such a term would not offend. I mean that the science itself consists of a stripped-down method and its findings, and that there must form around it not only a halo or encrustation of fictions, hypotheses, and non-empirically derived speculations, but also an attitudinal complex, rather like a system of illusions and delusions, or like a ruling formula (a term which Gaetano Mosca applied to the field of political science).

This auxiliary suprascience functions as a propaganda machine to make the science appear to its practitioners and public as continuously worthwhile, to tie it non-empirically into various problem areas of life, to act as a lightning rod (I will not argue whether lightning rods really are effective against lightning) to dissipate attacks gathering against the field, to give the field a history (much of it pseudo-history) and a future (much of the genre of science fiction).

As political science is impossible to consider without its ruling formulas (elites, democracy, kingship, laissez-faire, militarism, etc.), so astronomy cannot exist unaccompanied by schools of astrology, or geology without forms of uniformitarianism, or economics without models of "economic man," or literary analysis without fads and fashions, or medicine without magic and homeopathy, or chemistry without suprasciences, one or more for each of its numerous subdivisions such as diets alongside food chemistry, drug cultures alongside drugs, aesthetics alongside plastics, and so on.

There is no fakery here; there is strict necessity; man lives in the skies as well as in his hovel; culture marches along all paths and all paths are psychically connected, even when, especially in a scientific and pragmatic age, they may be, by an effort of will, separated for specialized solutions.

Under these circumstances, man lives throughout the cosmos, effectively. He lives pragmatically in the cosmos that he can experience and command through sensory manipulation. He lives mentally (and, by ritual, pragmatically) in the cosmos that is beyond experiencing but which he can imagine and bring into order. We may fancy that Jesus of Nazareth would speak this parable:

> A woman of the mountains saved her money to buy a rain cloak, for she was often wetted by the rains there, and when she had sufficient she ventured to Jerusalem to buy a cloak. But the cloak was so beautiful, that she would not wear it, so as to preserve it, and all her clothing became wet and damaged. Now I say unto you, wear your beautiful cloak of religion and all of your other clothing will be saved, and your Father in Heaven will replace your rain cloak with the raiment of angels.

Reason, many theologians and secularists pray, will serve religion, and show a person what is good and bad in religion. So, if there is bad religion, it is because men do not use their reason to find the good, or they exercise their free will to choose to do bad with religion.

Rationalism is thus used in two ways to damage religion. First, it becomes secular and refutes most or all religious pretension, as with Voltaire and Marx. Second, and more important here because it is a lesser known argument, rationalism erodes religion because it claims that mankind, possessed of the gift of telling what is "true" religion from what is "false" religion, only needs to be educated to distinguish "truth" in order to pursue true religion.

Thus the problems of religion can be said to be solved by the independent pursuit of the principles of reason with regard to supernatural beings and rituals. In this second situation, the rationalist theologians, counting here Saint Thomas Aquinas insofar as he is Aristotelian and rationalistic, lend themselves to the continuation of evil in the name of religion; for evil becomes the result of ignorance and neglect of reason.

Reason, as conceived in traditional and conventional philosophy and theology, presumes "free will." Free will is considered as the endowment of human nature with the capacity to choose one out of two or more alternative options as the basis for action upon an issue. Thus, employing reason, a choice of good over evil is imposed by free will, and an opposite decision becomes a free choice of evil. It is this "free will" which has been used in many cultures to explain the harsh effects of religion. Man is wicked and is therefore punished by his gods; by no means can the wickedness be blamed on the gods.

This argument would appear to constitute an imposing defense of traditional religion and may even explain why all other life

activities are dealt with by the principles of rationalism and free will
(rather than the other way around). If so, it is one more important
indication of the extent to which the religious sphere permeates and
dominates the structure and operations of the other seemingly
separated spheres of life.

Actually, the belief in free will can be viewed as a primary
obstacle to the improvement of religion. Not only does it make of
man in his own eyes a wicked sinner, much more fearful of the gods,
the authorities, and the people around him than he would otherwise
be, hence aggravating his natural paranoia, ambivalence, and hostility
to others. But it also makes it impossible for man to govern himself;
for he believes that he has within him, quite divorced from the really
essential set of mechanisms according to which he behaves, the
ability at any time to change himself from good to bad and from bad
from bad to good.

Furthermore, the "bad" and "good" are themselves applied in
the religious sphere often quite apart from any connections which
they might have with the other spheres of life. "Free will," and
rationalism as well, are fantastically individualistic fictions. They
permit the dissociation of an individual decision from all that in fact
determines, and should determine, the decision. Neither a balky
donkey nor the gods themselves can prevent man's exercising his will
upon them to turn along his way.

By contrast, the theory of *homo schizo* holds that man derives his
religion from the same set of mechanisms whence he derives all his
other interests and activities. One cannot allow the concepts of free
will and rationalism to enter. All of human behavior considered as a
mind transacting within himself and throughout the medium of his
culture is of one piece, holistic.

Free will is no longer, if it ever was, a useful idea. The known
and experienced deviations or range of choice available to us is large
enough, whether determined or free, to allow for extremely diverse
decisions.

Now see what this theory of *homo schizo* does to the status of
the supernatural and of religion. It elevates their status, rather than
depressing it. But, more than that, it makes sacred and religious man
impregnable to separatistic assaults upon his religion. For he can say
and he can prove, or others can do this for him, that even if his
religious aspects are suppressed, he will be different only in those

particulars where a transference occurs, from the prohibited areas of religion, to the permitted secular areas.

Religious man can further declare that the elimination of religion does not eliminate evil, but merely introduces more evil to other quarters of human behavior. And he can heap up evidence showing that secularized societies and secularized man have shown no noticeable improvement in conduct denominated as good.

Until we decide who we are and what we want to be, we are at fault in what we are and want to do. Unless we shut the doors against all unwanted conduct from all spheres of life, shutting the door against religion in the hope of stopping all unwanted conduct is futile; it will enter by the other doors. As well as saying that religion cannot be suppressed, and as well as stating that much of religious behavior is true both in itself and in reconciliation with science, we are now prepared to say that the suppression of religion will not consign evil beyond man's ken. For that great task, a reconstruction of human nature is required.

Such a reconstruction may well be impossible. We do not know enough yet to define the terms of reform. What we can do at this stage of our study is to argue for the incorporation into religion of our findings, both to prepare the ground for the possible coming reconstruction and to maintain the best possible, the least damaging, of religious as well as of all other systems.

The problem of absolute morality - of the standards of good conduct and the means to practice it - must go unsolved here. Absolute morality may be forever beyond human abilities to demonstrate. Short of this, we resort to what many philosophers before us have advocated, a natural law of human behavior: How people have always behaved and seem compelled to behave is restructured so that the consequences which people seem always to have wanted - even when acting in contradiction - will ensue.

Since we do not appeal to gods, reason, or secular authorities, nor to charism, faith, and revelation, it would appear best to label our natural law as hypothetical, tentative, and only so good as its consequences are acceptable to most people, whether educated or not, in all cultures. This might be called a natural moral consensus.

To summarize from suggestions offered in various passages of our work, we perceive four essential and general human demands: for freedom from fear, for material subsistence, for new experiences, and for a disinterested arbitration of human conflicts. Fearlessness; subsistence; experiencing; and justice: these words may be used also.

All of these require controls over the self (selves), others, and nature. Control requires skills (considering even brute force as a kind of skill at leverage, if nothing else), and mankind is obsessively driven to elaborate his internal and external control system to a stage where he has obtained what he can regard as minimal and sufficient guarantees of his several needs.

The overall problem of a culture is, unconsciously or consciously, to provide a network of practices that will supply its people with excellent chances of obtaining these guarantees. And so we proceed to human relations, technology, politics, religion - family government, world government, cosmic government – and science, which acts to supply better ways for cultures to fulfill these needs.

CHAPTER TWELVE

NEW PROOFS OF GOD

Ideas of quantavolution - of sudden great changes - attract the attention of historians of religion in especially two regards: religion was, and must remain in whatsoever guise, the companion of the newly born, traumatized, self-aware human mind; and the earliest religious voices, still speaking through the sacred documents of ancient times, were telling many truths, even literal truths about natural events, human nature, and human institutions - truths that bespeak quantavolutions.

Yet quantavolution also presents a distressing problem to those who believe that, if once they could approach closer to the earliest days, when "the gods walked on earth," they would be inspired, ennobled, and reinforced in their faith. This is not the case and they may well become downhearted and skeptical.

They should realize that even before quantavolution was assembled as a body of theories, those theologians, mystics and millennialists who ventured into the great first days of creation had to feel the terror and suffering that comes with "looking upon the face of god." Hence, indeed, most religions have calibrated the approaches to the sacred, so that only the well-prepared and thoroughly-warned would attempt the journey. That is, long before quantavolutionism, it was fully known that only the hardiest of souls could cope with the revelations of the first ages, could endure the historicity of the apocalypse.

It is possible to absorb the theories of quantavolution solely in the form of science, eschewing all contact with the religious experience as truth, while pursuing every avenue to religious experience as sociological and psychological fact. That is, quantavolution would only ask of its students that they exercise its hypotheses and evidence according to the current general methodology of science. This would be the more comfortable and easier choice.

Alternatively, however, one may confront the issue of the religious truth contained in this body of revolutionary theories, probing, inquiring whether perchance there is inherent in them something that those seeking a truth that is religious will recognize as valuable. The road is hard, and lined with the philosophical tombstones of many catastrophists and uniformitarians who have gone before, trying each in turn to transport a body of science into the realms of religious truth. Nevertheless I shall aim at the same goal.

I shall try to reach my goal in several steps. A metaphor of a box is used throughout. The human mind is inextricably contained within a physiologically limited box of perceptive possibilities and cyclical redundant logic.

The truths of religion are not within this box. Yet the existence of the box is proof of the supernatural, this being what is outside the box, which, we must admit, has an outside.

It is well that religious truths are not within this box, for the box limits and shapes its contents, and therefore disciplines the fields of knowledge that it holds.

The box nevertheless is indefinitely expansible. Its resources and limits have not been fully tested or strained. (This differs from the expansion mentioned above, which was only communicative expansion.)

In whatever direction the box expands, it is not likely to be limited. Hence the supernatural is not bounded by the accomplished full testing of any of its facets.

The simplicity and complexity of things are subjectively perceived or operationally invented. Things in themselves cannot be defined as absolutely simple or complex. The same is true of the concepts of space (size), time, past, and future.

The same is true of "life" or "animism." It is subjective percept or operational invention, not defined other than by the human mind.

Now, if god is whatever is beyond the box (i. e. limitless), god must be also what is in the box, inasmuch as what is in the box is speculating upon what is outside of it, as we here.

Therefore, all that we sense and think in ourselves and our perceptible and thinkable world is part of the supernatural. If the supernatural and god are joined, we are pantheists.

Putting god into an animistic metaphor, god is our judge; god has already judged us. We already are composed and function according to god's cosmic spirit, by intelligence, and necessity.

The very nature of our ignorance, then, cribbed and confined in our cosmic box, constitutes a proof of the existence of gods. The agreement of extended ignorance from the crypto-blind bio-box probably stands up better under modern scrutiny than the traditional arguments for the proof of god that we mentioned in an earlier chapter.

Furthermore, a second modern proof may tend to confirm the existence of gods, and support the proof from the cosmic box.

The universe is presently thought to be some billions of years old, probably finite, although the boundaries are not clear, and populated by many billions of stars. Many stars, if not most of them, are believed to have spawned planets. Planets will have had ample occasion to acquire atmospheres and "the building blocks of life," as we like to say from inside our cosmic box. We are also forced to admit that life as we know it is defined from inside our box, and "intelligence," as we might conceive it without actually knowing it, may be a product of other means of manufacture and assembly.

Even if we have to conjecture the birth of gods from the elements of the atomic table, the combinations and permutations of this, plus the practically unlimited conditions of time, space, temperature, and pressure can provide the substance and form of a god whom even scientific materialists, even Karl Marx, could recognize as authentic and in being.

In the creation of all things, we must contend with the principle of entropy, a term invented by Clausius in 1865 to refer to the state in which thermal energy is no longer available for mechanical work. Later, and especially with Norbert Wiener, the term was broadened to describe "the running down of the universe." Clausius himself had written "the entropy of the universe tends to a maximum." (Thus the idea merely subsisted until a century of history changed the optimistic mid-nineteenth to the pessimistic mid-twentieth century intellectual climate.)

Given even a time of short duration, or of a conventional dozen billion solar years, the number of occasions for "phenomena" or "phenomenal intelligence" to appear in the universe is extremely large. Cases of "negative entropy," that is, of existence moving toward creation rather than desuetude, must be very numerous.

There is no reason to use life on earth as the archetype of the universe. As the *Encyclopaedia Britannica* reports, "all the organisms of the earth are extremely closely related, despite superficial differences. The fundamental ground pattern, both in form and flesh, of all life on earth is essentially identical." Nor ought we take mankind as the measure of the product of potential habitats of intelligence. In some proportion of them, something much more than *homo sapiens schizotypus* must have emerged. There should exist planets or complexes where beings of much greater intelligence and competence than ourselves exist. There must be a range of such superior intelligences from superman to gods.

Whether individuals, conglomerates, complexes, spirits, physiological aggregations unknown to us, or even creatures suggesting ourselves, these will all have many times our abilities. Perhaps some will have supernatural capacities (for we cannot understand them) a billion times our own. Perhaps one of the beings may have generated power to move the universe itself; for, as the second law of thermodynamics maintains that the universe and all matter within it is running down, but an exception is made in the case of life which is negatively entropic, so there is an excellent chance that somewhere in the universe is an intelligent being, of which we can conceive but which we cannot become, whose powers are such that it is in control of the universe, moving in the direction of intelligence and progress as we conceive of it: this being certainly must be called god. It would then be for all practical purposes omniscient and omnipotent. That it would be all-caring, omni-benevolent, may also be presumed, for to take care of itself it would have to take care of the universe in some part, as a case of "enlightened selfishness," in our limited human terminology.

Thus the traditional concept of god is exercised with a new proof involving the probability of supreme negative entropy. God is created by the universe, working in opposition to the principle of entropy with the equally universal principle of creation. The creative principle, arising like the phoenix from its ashes of entropy, must naturally turn to controlling the universe.

If this god is not already a fact, still, in the aeons of time to come, it must become a certainty. As the local gods of the solar system were born and died in succession, there may have been many temporary or quasi-omnipotent gods in times and spaces beyond all solar system experience. The universe offers billions of chances for a supreme god to arise in the future. Sooner or later, the universe will create its supreme master, just as the earth, this indescribably minute place, has created its locally supreme master, the human. Whereupon truly the universe would be intelligently ordered, as contrasted with the present chaos, and the far-flung parts, including our own, would be irresistibly induced to cooperate.

Let us proceed to discuss this theory of divine actual or potential existence at greater length.

To establish a new religion on solid grounds requires that the history of religion as the history of the true god be rejected. If one relies upon the scientific history of religion, one would be led to the conclusion that gods do not exist. Luckily for those who yearn for gods, one can go beyond the history of religion, to psychology and philosophy. There they will learn that the human mind is basically limited. Its perceptions and condition are structurally bounded. To exceed this structure, they must rely only upon corollaries of the cosmic proof: 1) extension of some hitherto neglected remote recesses of the structure of mind and body and 2) a type of reasoning that proceeds on an "if.... then" basis which says: This is desirable; the question is open; the desirable is therefore not foreclosed. If god exists or gods, and is as we think god ought to be, then we are happier and can seek progress. Since the "if" cannot be foreclosed by any known means, the "then" is always possible.

What is greater than the self can only be known anthropomorphically, that is, by extensions of the self as it is known to one. Hence, if the universe has dimensions that are quite divorced from human traits (or their extensions), we can never know them. But the premise that more exists, which we cannot possibly know, is itself a proof of the existence of gods, even though we cannot know them in any other way than in this paltry manner. Moreover, it is possible that dimensions of the universe hitherto unknowable to us will make themselves known, whether because they change so as to be comprehensible (" God makes himself known,") or we change ourselves structurally by genetic accident or manipulation.

If the universe has only those qualities which we now possess or may in the future possess, or if the universe changes its qualities, then we can come to a knowledge of the gods that we, in our limited way, know must be there.

Are these possibilities of knowledge additive? Can we say that our full knowing potential *plus* the potential of the unknown gives us virtual certainty that gods exist? Like the lost sailor, we know that land lies in every direction. Also, we know that land may be far away if we go in some directions. Can we determine in what direction the divine land lies?

A wee mouse, five centimeters long, is in many ways superior to the human. In proportion to size, he can run 20 times as fast, jump fifty times as high, scale walls, swim naturally well, has senses superior to those of men, and trains readily for reactive tasks. His brain and his organs are marvels of miniaturization, relative to ourselves. The outstanding difference is that homo is schizotypical, that is, self-aware and all that flows from this fact.

We know nothing about any species that has the equivalent of schizotypicality and what this affords us. We can conjecture how many species in all the universe might be schizotypical or have other systems capable of performing operations that we designate as being along the parameter of the human-as-divine up to the exceedingly divine, that is, the full god.

Moses and his followers claimed that Yahweh could see and punish malefactors and delinquents. The Christian religion says that God can know the minds of all persons. Paranoids will sometimes say that they can tell what all minds in a crowd are thinking and single out individual minds, too. A body containing 10^{20} cells can pass a signal to most or perhaps all cells in a brief time so that they are all reacting consonantly. The number of Jews is 10^7+, of Christians 10^9, of humans 4×10^9. The coordination of "nature" exceeds that of gods, so to say, in some respects, and goes far beyond the most paranoid human mind. (Indeed, many humans are content to control one other person, such as a spouse or child.) Coordination means two things: *communication and control.*

Thus far, the shocking modern revelation of the numberless stars and vast extent of the universe has been converted into constructive thought regarding the possibility of there being other intelligent beings in the universe, with whom we might possibly communicate. Inevitably the thought has been elaborated into contentions that at some time in the past, astronauts have settled upon our planet, assimilating biologically with lesser breeds, or constituting the human race itself. The thought has also moved, theoretically, to the contention that more intelligent or hostile or flagrantly incompatible beings might be confronted, to our embarrassment, should we be successful in communicating with exoterrestrials.

These discussions employ formulas not essentially different from what we employ here. We take up estimates of 10^{11} galaxies of 10^{11} stars each, without counting dark stars or clouds, reaching thus 10^{22} stars. We count 10^{22} dark stars and dark clouds as having theogonic possibilities (" darkness" is our problem). Gods take time to develop, but we may assume that the average body has had enough of such time, billions of years. Whether, for instance, the Earth has subsisted for 4×10^{9} or 10^{6} years, it has had at least a 10^{44} possibility of generating a god. Of the total source bodies, some 10^{11} (plus dark stars and clouds) would exist in our galaxy alone. We are not counting the separate planets or comets, that would multiply these several stellar figures by 2, 5, 500, 1,000 or some other multiple not known, but depending on the average number of planets per star.

Suppose that science on Earth expands its capabilities ten times, a figure not in excess of many predictions from various fields. Suppose the human achieves an IQ of 160, lives to be 200, and can travel to the neighboring star cluster of Arcturus. Suppose the human is even morally set upon acting as god. The human will probably not be a god, but he will show that gods are possible somewhere. That is, it does not take too much more than man can be in order to define a god or demigod.

If there also are and have been 5×10^{11} centers for realizing divine beings in the galaxy and this over a period of time - in fact, why not infinity? - then the chance that one or more gods have developed is certain. Probabilistically, at least one is certain; let us say five are highly probable; 5,000 are likely; 5 million are at least 50% probable; and some 50 million gods are possible, this in our galaxy alone. In the universe as a whole, these figures would be multiplied by 10^{22}. At 5,000 per galaxy, the gods would number 5×10^{25}, too many by far to crowd into Valhalla. If gods should die (speaking of the *Götterdammerung*), that is, lose some or all of their capabilities, one would halve the number of gods in the confines of the stipulated universe.

Among all of the probable godships, should not many have evolved to a multi-galactic god, and at least one to supreme god of the universe? An interesting feature of the results here is that there appear to have been more gods than the conventional formulas claim there to be planets with intelligent life forms. This paradox occurs because one does not constrain estimates by looking for something close to man, to technical civilization, or intelligent life as we know it. Further the requirements of an environment similar to man's can be waived; the gods need not be limited by humanly severe temperatures, or the presence of a long string of prior primitive life forms called for by non-quantavolutionary evolution.

Thus, as soon as less conservative considerations than are customary are set for intelligent forms in the universe, the number quickly exceeds the number of gods estimated here. Ordinary calculations of life spans are irrelevant, too; the occurrence of gods presumptively reduces time constraints; the possibility of divine viability stretching over much, most or all of the age of the universe adds to the probability that gods are active now.

In sum, of the terms of the formula used in many discussions of communication with extraterrestrial intelligence (CETI), only the gross number of celestial bodies is usable in estimating the likelihood of the existence of gods. To find the number of extant technical civilizations in the galaxy, by the "Green Bank formula" of F. D. Drake, N, one multiplies R^* (the average rate of star formation over the lifetime of the galaxy), by f_p (the fraction of stars with planetary systems), by n_o (the mean number of planets per star that are ecologically suitable for the origin of life as we know it), by f_e (the fraction of such planets on which life in fact has arisen), by f_i (the fraction of such planets on which intelligent life has evolved), by f_c (the fraction of such planets on which a technical civilization such as our own has developed) and by L (the average life of a technical civilization). That is, $N = R^* (f_p)(n_o)(f_e)(f_i)(f_c)(L)$.

Results, depending upon the estimates fed into the formula, have ranged from one to millions of technical civilizations in the galaxy. Our own technical civilization capable of interstellar radio communication is only a single generation old. The 1000-foot-diameter telescope at Arecibo Observatory in Puerto Rico, existing transmitters and receivers, and a presumption of the same type of equipment on another planet would provide a communication medium of 1000 light-year diameter, providing 10^6 stars. Space travel and laser transmission are technically near availability to extend somewhat the range. There is therefore some chance of a communication exchange now.

But how have we defined a god that gods should be so numerous? By god is meant a coordinated divine activity such that 1) it can endure or reproduce or replicate itself indefinitely under highly varying ambient conditions, that 2) it can act so as to expand communication pathways and thus its influence at an exponentially increasing rate, that 3) its proven scope and domain of intervention is extensive within a galaxy or is multigalactic, and contains no inherent limits, that 4) it provably (in human terms) acts so as to increase the aptitude and appropriate behaviors of the most promising existences (including humans) with the end in mind of reducing entropy and establishing theotropy as the dominating principle of the universe.

How do these qualities, if applied to the human condition, reduce fear, war, and famine, while increasing love and knowledge? I have mentioned but a few of such moral connections in these pages. Their deduction from the principles of godship do not appear to present problems in excess of those traditionally and successfully solved by theologians such as Saint Thomas Aquinas when deducing human moral behavior from the qualities of gods.

Theotropy can be considered from the standpoint of gods and of humans. Regarding gods, the achievement of influence is by means and in terms that we understand or cannot understand. So far as we can understand, gods must extend themselves either immediately or by a succession of moves.

Insofar as our world is governed by no intelligent divine influence – then no god has even in our short-time view extended itself over us, whereupon we can probably more correctly imagine that any god occupying itself with humans is proceeding by a succession of moves, that is, by growth. Both may be occurring, a onetime immediate assumption of our world and a succession of moves to change us.

A reader who has pursued our works on quantavolution knows how we believe man to have acquired his nature and how the world as we know it has come about. Thereupon he may ask: "Why does man need a god, considering all the troubles gods have appeared to cause?" Worse, "What legitimate reason has man for seeking god?"

Worse of all, "What can any god do for man that is good for man?"

First of all, none of these questions can destroy the gods if they do indeed exist. No more than one can dispose of tax collectors who are troublesome and unwanted. From a homocentric point of view, however, we can be more cooperative in responding.

We need all the help we can get, plainly and simply. We are inadequate to our dearest wishes for the universe: that it be controlled and beneficent to ourselves and the posterity with which we identify.

We need help of a quality that is beyond the ability of everything whose qualities we know directly. Our faithful dog, Shep, is not up to the task. Nor are even our most trusted friends and allies. If there is a god, we need him.

The third question gives us pause. If the price exacted by seeking, finding and cooperating with god is our most priceless gifts, we may prefer our troubles, death, entropy, and oblivion. This leads abruptly to the question which we seem to confront us at every turn of the way. What does, what ought, the human wish to be? If he wishes to be like the gods, and the gods are likely to be so indulgent, then all is well and good, and we should search eternally, if necessary, for the gods.

One's purpose on Earth will then be answered from the divine point of view: the human is created for the divine task of helping to save the universe. He, and all developing and positive matter, are assigned this overall function. The universe has bred the human as a way to its own survival, as a challenge to its death, as an antibody against the death and dissolution foretold by the second law of thermodynamics.

Elsewhere we have written of man's basic needs, to fearlessly subsist, experience and live justly. If the gods are theotropic, we have nothing to fear from them except the loss of that element in us which is self-destructive and entropic.

What might this element be? Let us call it the diabolic, because it will turn out to be that often highly attractive mixture of uncertainty, fear, hatred, spite, lies, greed and egotism that goes into some of the most wonderful human creations. Will not the gods take from man the taste of evil for which he slavers? Or will the gods, like certain historical gods, allow man the gift of diabolism with all that it does for his music, dance, art, inventions, and politics?

This is one question; another question, equally important, is related: will the gods take away self-government, self-rule, decentralization of decisions, whether large or small? There is indeed an argument, posed as, "Let every man go to hell in the own way." The felt uniqueness, the exultation, the happiness of determining one's way are not to be given over, even to the gods, one senses - and we can hear the most stupid as well as the most brilliant of humans saying so.

Perhaps the gods will be indifferent to such trivialities, perhaps they work sloppily, letting as much as we know of life pursue itself along their general guidelines. Or perhaps it will happen that in their intense pursuit of godliness, humans will get their fill of risks, conflicts, imagination, and autonomy. In any event, this crisis is far down the line of theotropy, whereas man's decline and destruction are always close at hand. We prefer to think therefore that, in the pursuit of the divine, humanity will have all that it will want of symbolism, diversity, and excitement.

From the human standpoint, gods are to be awaited and solicited. If they are awaited, the presumption is that the gods are interested in expansion for its own sake. Any part to the universe will do. This is probably an unsafe assumption because it implies a certain kind of god. But god is more than a mere "land-grabber," we reason. He is interested in his own development; he is maximizing his opportunities of theotropy and not interested in entropic refuse. Therefore, gods are to be invited. For some lucky mystics, gods may indeed already have been entertained. I cannot understand the means, hence cannot confirm the encounters.

But what are the occasions for conflict among potential and actual gods in the galaxy and universe prior to the universal achievement of a single supreme god? Will there not occur what even mankind has experienced on its low level of achievement, a set of squabbling barons, a battle of the gods? Then the gods themselves will do what it is now widely believed that man will do - destroy themselves and contribute to the entropy of the universe? As they move out to order and exalt the universe, what will determine their jurisdictions and, as implied in their aims, will merge them into one?

Let us look once again at the traits of the divine bodies. They excel in expansiveness, in sensitivity to domains of potential theotropic existence, and in promoting theotropism (countering entropy). It is this last that determines outcomes. The theotropism or divinity that competes most effectively to eliminate entropy will merge with other divinities to the degree that they operate in the same way. It is to their interest to behave in this way. In the end it will be the constructive principle of the universe that will influence and absorb all potential theotropy in the universe. Creation will triumph over destruction. This is the aim of the universe, the greatest of natural laws, and is the ultimate good.

A second objection occurs. If, as has been asserted in this work, man is not a rational animal in any usual sense of the term "reason," and if sublimation is employed to move him from his great fear of himself and the world into large intellectual, imaginative and real worlds far beyond himself, then why is this proof of the existence of divinity not another sublimatory consideration? Is this all "mere" sublimation?

The answer is that sublimation is not unreal, even though it may refuse to treat directly with its origins in human nature. Its rationalizations are testable by rules of reality, logic, consensus, pragmatism, and evidence; this, too, we have said earlier, and will discuss later as well. Granted this, the theotropic proof must contend with all other assertions about divinity on the basis of which ones best fit the state of the world as we barely know it and of whatever provides the best consequences for the human condition. *Homo sapiens schizotypus* is released from his fearful bind and contradictions by this view of the supernatural and is directed to employ his energies constructively – theotropically, rather than entropically.

If the principle of entropy exists - and we think that this is so out of our material perceptions - then its opposite principle may exist because, first, the world is not fully entropic, next, there is an anti-entropism observed, and, third, entropism must originate from something that decays. In this last case, the something that decays must have been non-entropic, possibly anti-entropic, that is, theotropic.

The entropy and theotropy can co-exist: they do so under our eyes. It may appear that the theotropic is declining, but this may be false. Our narrow perspective may be giving false measures, and we are better conditioned to detect entropy than theotropy. Especially with our present confidence in materialism, that is, our indifference to theotropy and our desire to emulate the ideal instinctive animal, we may be today underestimating theotropy.

But is not the theotropic also material? It can properly be conceived as such, but only if we realize that most of what we call material is the refuse of theotropic materialism. As to what composes theotropic processes, we submit that theotropy is composed of what is tangibly material, of some extremes of the knowably material (particles, waves, light, etc.) of material potentially known to us but not yet known, and of material unknowable to us. I only call it material for fear of erecting barriers between the "material" and "immaterial."

Under the regime of theotropy, it appears that mankind is to be more of an observer, thinker and admirer of the abstract than the active being who is acted upon. How can he behave religiously otherwise, and how can his morals connect with this religion?

First, one who possesses this religion will be occupied with the future, as historical man has first sought a heavenly salvation and lately has sought salvation in the future also, but in a more scientific and technological way.

Second, he will be more objectively self-searching and theological than historically he has been. He is looking for a different kind of divinity; this affects the quality of the search.

Thirdly, he has to consider the question: Do I wish to attract gods? Do I wish to be adopted by gods, lightning-struck so to speak; do I wish to become chosen by the gods? Do I wish to be embraced by a larger theotropy than I have means of becoming in myself??

Surprisingly the answer to all of these questions will be a strong affirmative. (I say surprisingly for I feel personally that we have no right to expect such definite answers to questions that we have formulated with such difficulty and hesitation.)

Behind the banners of entropism stands a sad, scientoid diabolism. We do want to live in theotropy, in the future, in the realms of the gods.

Then the question becomes: How do we attract the gods? Do we do so with signals, search parties on vehicles, sending care packages of our little technical tricks into outer space?

Or do we go seeking the gods with a message that we think will have meaning for them? What could such a message be?

Our best message, our invitation to the gods, is our ability to take care of our own world and its surroundings. It stands to reason that the gods, if they have already reached us actually or potentially, or if they were to come upon us in their expanding operations in the universe, would either embrace us or dismiss us by indifference or destruction.

What would achieve their embrace? Obviously, they would embrace theotropy, for that is their essence. What are the signs of theotropy, which in our older language we might call blessedness? They would have to be signs of which we are capable. These signs are not negligible; they are signs of godliness.

Theotropy is the trend of existence to achieve divine influence. Inasmuch as humans may be capable of it, it calls for an expansion of the influence of life over death and of mind over matter. Thus, it appears that the very principles that we have ascribed to the theotropy of the gods are principles that reverberate down the corridors of human time and thought.

If these principles go unattended or are unsuccessfully pursued by mankind, the gods will not punish us; the gods have more important matters on their more universal "minds." They will ignore us, and let us continue in the predictable shortness of our forever to suffer both from our own behavior and being god-forsaken, which must mean the loss of our hopes, of our development, and of our future.

There are a great many people who believe that god may exist but always has reason to punish people, so much so that it is useless to attempt even a decent peaceful and material subsistence for mankind. Famine, plague, flood or war are seen to be inevitable divine visitations. Such apathy and fatalism go along with the succession of gods who could hardly allow mankind to recover from one catastrophe before bringing down another upon it.

At the other extreme of materialism stands the vanguard of the technical achievers. So flushed are they with the successes of empirical science, that they predict a never-ending invigoration of life and conquest of vast reaches of outer space. Among these are the ones who would fill capsules with gimcracks to fire into far space.

The fatal flaw in their vision and plans is a misperception of human limits. The human race stands at a crisis of will and belief, of world disintegration and warfare, even as vehicles hurtle into outer space. Humans have not solved their basic issues of life over death, and mind over matter. They may be incapable of doing so without the help of a greater theotropy than they can neurologically possess. The most that they may be capable of, and it would indeed be a great achievement, is to invite the gods for help on matters of life and mind. This the technocrats and military operators of the political economy and outer space are of no mind to do, whether they by acting in the name of mosaism or atheism. In their arrogance, they see no need to invite the gods to their feast. Or they try to beckon to them by exercises paralleling the long history of sacrificed beings and the destruction of nations.

We conclude that gods - or god, if you will - exist. They do not exist in fear; fear is human alone. They exist in our mind as the mind tests the limits of reality and invents, while integrating these limits, a special kind of reality in the supernatural - the area of the divine. Gods exist outside the mind with as much probability as the universe that we contemplate is real. In these two senses, god is reality.

Granted reality, the divine must be our most important reality. This may seem to be skating on the thin ice of scholasticism. "Tell it to a starving man." But it is a statistical reality and in the final analysis it is statistics that compose reality of all kinds. The divine is the most important because it is the only distinction that is uniquely human; it comes straight out of the awful realization of one's divided soul, two or more material contradictions, ineradicable and appositionally creative.

Climactically, a reconciliation takes place in philosophy and science. To know oneself is to know more than oneself; it is to know the divine. Here is the reason for the failure of historical religions, which damaged the soul is order to force it to hold delusions about "hard reality" and external gods at the same time.

CHAPTER THIRTEEN

CATECHISM

A catechism can summarize the fundamental facts and doctrines of religion from our perspective. The word "catechism", which now broadly means an elementary instruction manual in a given field, has for seventeen hundred years meant, more precisely, exercises for instructing Christian neophytes. Before the word achieved popularity in its Latinized Greek form, it may have come from the combined words "tying down", connoting a binding divine covenant. Less religiously, it recalls a metaphorical American usage of the same words, as when we "tie down" a matter so as to put it in form for easy handling. Our catechism here intends to tie down in a well-known format the basic facts and doctrines of religion deriving from our study.

Setting forth a catechism exposes to a pitiless light our beliefs concerning religion. The onus of proselytism comes with it, for a catechism must tell people what they should believe. There are health and strength in such an exercise.

KNOWLEDGE

1. *How was the universe created?*
    The world has always existed in some of its infinitely possible manifestations, and is being created in some others today, and so it will go on.

2. *How long will this Earth endure?*
   The Earth will endure for an inestimable time, depending upon mostly unpredictable natural, and divine human events.

3. *How much can a person know about the world?*
   One can know more than one can learn and much less than what exists.

4. *Can one know oneself?*
   One can know oneself within the limits of one's abilities to know oneself.

5. *Are the limits of these abilities known and achievable?*
   The limits of the abilities to know oneself are unknown but more extensive than the abilities anyone has shown.

6. *What should a person know of oneself?*
   One should appreciate one's operative complex of self-controls.

7. *Does a person have free will?*
   One acts in accord with one's nature and circumstances; free will as action in ignorance of one's nature and circumstances can exist, but is not characteristic of an autonomous rational person.

8. *What is known absolutely?*
   Nothing that matters. The absolute should be ignored because its main function is to promote absolute fear.

9. *What is absolutely clear?*
   Nothing, and tolerance of ambiguity should be a religious principle, both to combat fear and to express the supernatural.

10. *What is science?*
    Science may be usefully defined as the method of choosing the largest chance of certainty in solving problems whose conditions and objectives are known.

11. *How should science relate to religion?*
    Science should solve an increasingly large number of the indefinitely large number of problems of religion, while religion expresses some of the directives and limits of science.

12. *How should we express our relation to the cosmos?*
    We should relate to the cosmos by understanding it and celebrating it.

MORALS

13. *What needs has one?*
    One's needs are fearlessly to subsist, to experience, and to be treated justly.
14. *What duties has one?*
    One's duties are to help others fearlessly to subsist, to experience, and to be justly treated.
15. *Who is divine among people?*
    Whoever studies and expresses the divine is divine.
16. *What differences exist between means and ends?*
    A means is a process of action that contributes to a more general process of action; it is rational according to how it works; it is deemed good or bad in its own effects and therefore contributes more or less good or bad to the end process.
17. *Is good rewarded?*
    Insofar as the religious and secular realms are consonant, good action is rewarded in both; the rewards of religion should be in its practice and in the health of character that it fosters.
18. *Should evil be punished?*
    Evil should be compensated for, personally and socially, not punished; it should be treated as a problem of coping with natural forces.
19. *Do right and wrong belong in the realm of the gods?*
    Yes, they belong where the human and divine realms interact.
20. *Can a person distinguish right and wrong?*
    Yes, by exercising himself in the fringes of the supernatural realm where the mundane realm fashions its judgments.
21. *What is right or wrong?*
    Right is a determination of consistency in the consequences of an action with the divine aspect of a person.
22. *By what rules should a person act?*
    A person should act by the rules of one's nature adjusted to the related ordinances of a consensus of like-minded others.
23. *How should a person behave toward oneself?*
    One should accommodate consistently one's divine and mundane character.

24. *How should a person behave towards others?*

One should act towards others as to a differently shaped development of oneself, hence part of oneself, hence considerately, hence helpfully.

25. *How should a person behave toward plants and animals?*

One should behave toward plants and animals as toward others, while recognizing in them an acute differentiation from oneself in the tragic divine need to derive instinctive gratification from their exploitation.

26. *How should a person behave toward natural objects?*

As toward animals and plants, in descending series of their divinity.

27. *How should a person behave toward the supernatural?*

One should practice an understanding of its potential.

28. *What morality is devoid of religious significance?*

All morality should be religiously and politically promoted.

29. *What morality should be religiously and politically promoted?*

Morality should be promoted which comes from a constitution that is based upon consensus and offering procedures that among other effects tend to establish the dominion of divinity in humans.

30. *Is a person without religion bound to be wrong and evil?*

His views are narrow and he may not understand his own religiousness, but his actions may neither err nor have bad consequences.

31. *What function does a person serve in the world?*

The person represents and takes part in universal manifestations.

THE SUPERNATURAL AND DIVINE

32. *Is there a supernatural part of the world?*

What one cannot perceive and what one cannot understand, even if he learns something about it, is the supernatural.

33. *Is the supernatural divine?*

The supernatural is divine insofar as it is meaningfully integrated into human mentation, but divinity implies no superiority over the pragmatically knowable.

34. *What is the divine on Earth?*
The divine on Earth is a uniquely human way of looking upon oneself and the world.

35. *How does one worship the divine?*
The rituals for worshiping the divine are whatever exercises are useful to achieve it.

36. *What is sacred?*
Everything viewed in its supernatural and divine manifestations is sacred.

37. *What is faith?*
Faith is positive morale, a conviction of meaningfulness about what one is thinking and doing, which when related to the divine is religious faith.

38. *What is revelation?*
Revelation is the recognition by an internal or external stimulus of an important pattern to existence, not previously experienced, to which if a divine element is present, the term "religious" can be attached.

39. *What is discovery?*
Discovery is a revelation purposefully brought about, whose applications are readily apparent and available to others.

40. *What should authority be?*
Authority should be the legitimate power of one person over another, which may be religious; it should receive its legitimacy by the consensus of those ruled and should lose its legitimacy to the extent to which it is physically and mentally coercive.

41. *How should we behave toward the sacred?*
As toward the mundane, although, as with mundane varieties, we should act toward the sacred appropriately in accord with its distinctions.

42. *How much of our energies should be given to the divine?*
As much as necessary in order to receive divine energies in return, from ourselves, others, the world and gods.

43. *What is divine energy?*
Divine energy is the morale that comes from developing relations with the supernatural.

44. *Is there a sacred community?*
Yes, the community of those whose understanding of the divine is similar in forms, scope and intensity.

45. *Will the cosmos ever be divine?*

The theotropic universe will ultimately dominate the entropic universe.

46. *Is the divine also god?*

Yes, insofar as its mental integration functions as a presentation of the human mind, the divine is godly.

47. *To what futures should a person relate?*

A person chooses and lives partially in whatever futures one wants and is capable of participating in, except that upon death one's future is resolved into the cosmos and reconstructed beyond personal minding and control.

GODS

48. *Is it proper to expect gods?*

It is proper to expect gods, as it is to expect enlightenment.

49. *What is a god?*

A god is a generalized and immanent being, manifesting itself in material ways and through a demonstrable external cosmic spirit, operating in the human mind as the repository of the supernatural.

50. *Is god material existence?*

All material is effective: insofar as the divine is effective existence, and existence is all material, the divine is material, and so is god.

51. *Where is god?*

The god is wherever it can be and acts so as to be.

52. *Is there one god or many?*

There are both one and many gods, depending upon how the mind assembles the divine facets in its behavior.

53. *Do gods behave like humans?*

Yes, but only as the human in its universal and supernatural aspects.

54. *How many gods exits?*

We have not discovered how many, if any, gods exist on Earth, while in the universe myriad gods exist.

55. *What proofs do we have that there exists a supernatural, a divine, and a god?*

That divine beings exist is known by the logical extension of our ignorance and limitations into areas where divinity must begin and exist.

56. *Do all gods have the same traits and behavior?*
   Traits and behavior are limited ideas and actions to which the gods cannot be bound.

57. *Where is god in relation to the human?*
   The god is where the human mind is affected by the supernatural and the divine, or may ultimately be in conscious contact with it.

58. *How is a person related to god?*
   Personally, as to an aspect of oneself, socially as to a joint aspect of oneself and others.

59. *Does a person elect god?*
   A person chooses god but his election is jointly with others to the extent that the gods of others permit a joint representation.

60. *Can I will against gods?*
   One can will against gods entropically for self or universally, including reductionism to greater instinctive animality.

61. *Can all historical gods be attributed to catastrophes and other natural causes?*
   All historical gods are in at least some of their manifestations catastrophic.

62. *Are gods historical?*
   Historical gods have been the outcome of persons interacting with events, and, though probably non-existent, persist in some of their earlier manifestations, so that all are partly gone and partly present.

63. *Should a person obey historical gods in their original ascribed apparitions?*
   The gods of the past are to be treated as hypothetical models to avoid and imitate as they reflect upon the present and future and satisfy today's conditions of existence.

64. *Are the gods rational and welcome?*
   Insofar as they are theotropic rather than entropic, the gods are rational and welcome, and are to be preferred.

RELIGION

65. *Can society hold together without religion?*
   Society cannot be conceived without religion and therefore cannot hold together without it.

66. *Should two persons have the same religion?*

No two persons can have or should have the same religion; all religion is therefore personal.

67. *How are persons united by religion?*

Persons sharing significant religious perspectives identify with each other and constitute a church if they recognize their mutual identity.

68. *How should we regard existing religions?*

We should regard existing religions as in large part historically invalidated in terms of the ongoing and future historical process of religion, and encourage their voluntary assimilation and development into current standards of validation.

69. *Should there be priests?*

Priesthood as religious leadership must exist, and should be practiced ideally by all when they can, and by the fewest possible full time forever.

70. *What gifts should religion bring?*

Religion should bring joy of thought, wonderful awe, a divine community, and freedom from fear.

71. *What gifts should be made to religion?*

One should give to others by devotion, rituals, and cooperation the intelligence afforded by religion.

72. *What does religion offer to human suffering of body and mind?*

Religion offers to the suffering body and mind the knowledge of self, morale, scientific pragmatic support, and a cosmic sense of proportion.

73. *What symbols should be sacred?*

Symbols that retain the least historical implications and represent the major points of this catechism should be created and promoted and become subjects of admiration and stimulation; present sacred symbols should be reduced in significance and intensity.

74. *What are sacred scriptures?*

All graphic and written material that was ever sacred is still sacred and worthy of wonder and study, but at a reduced level of psychic investment, while new contributions intended as sacred scriptures should be no more sacred than any other sacrally intended or scientific or literary work for which merit is claimed.

75. *Should our rites be simple or elaborate?*
    Rituals should be as elaborate as necessary to learn the purpose of
    the ritual, as stressed as necessary to enjoy its reassurances, as
    simple as the available energies would afford, and should be
    productive of other goods aesthetically and otherwise.
76. *What is the educative task of religion?*
    Religion should educate people theotropically, which is the
    constructive life force.
77. *What is the task of politics?*
    The task of politics is the same as religion morally, but politics
    contends largely with the pragmatic problems issuing from
    theotropism.
78. *To what extend should we be bound by our religion?*
    We should be bound to our religion to the extent and so long as
    it helps us fulfill our obligations to ourselves and the world.
79. *How long will it be before humanity becomes religious?*
    Mankind will become religious when it discovers the existence of
    gods on experiential principles without delusion.

CONCLUSION

THE DIVINE AND HUMAN

Having begun with a pessimistic understanding of the divine succession, I have concluded with an optimistic belief that the search for the supernatural is a virtuous, healthy, and constructive activity. The divine exists and can be achieved to a significant degree by all who properly seek it. It is probable that the divine extends to the existence of gods, regarding whom the question of one or many is probably nonsense and should certainly not be sloganized.

Religion is the system of relations sought for and maintained among the humans and the divine, the divine being more extensive than the human. Religion or religiousness is morally effective and can often change secular behavior with beneficial effects upon human life and the satisfaction of human needs. Rituals are exercises of the human character and are beneficial in the context of a proper religion.

The search for religion is the most civilizing and lofty human experience; the claim to have found religion has been usually a disaster. Religion came with the first kit of mankind, mentally and physically. Religion covered all existence and does so even today and will do so. Neither the purely secular nor the purely sacral type of person is suited either to study or to maintain the divine search.

Secularism has never been fully accomplished because it contradicts itself when it reaches its psychic and moral origins. As the method of secularism, science can help greatly sacral man achieve the divine, provided that it accepts the help of theotropical theology.

Historical religions, based upon the terrible power of natural forces, limited strictly the extent to which humanity could pursue divinity. The gods were born as disastrous natural occurrences playing upon the existential fear of the self-aware human.

The theory of quantavolution explains, thus, substantially the history of religion and culture. It strengthens the scientific basis of religion by cutting off the claims of traditional religion to authorize personal miracles and to arrange divine intervention. Quantavolution furthermore discerns and pursues the consistent delusional schizoid syndrome of human nature from its beginnings. It explains the unbreakable connection between the sacred and secular.

Still, varieties of historical religions, such as Platonism, Stoicism, Christianity, Buddhism, and Bahai, have often approached the divine by the same routes as we have ourselves. They enlarged the human perspective and performed experiments; they organized social and intellectual infrastructures for launches into the future.

The goal of religious practice is the revelation of the divine through the human, and the integration of the human with the universally divine. This aim, which may be infinite and unachievable, promotes operations extending beyond the blinded box in which the human mind must work and seeks to establish relations with divine probabilities wherever they may exist and be sensed.

The world of entropy is the dying universe of the second law of thermodynamics, and of the dying mind. Entropy is confronted and contradicted by theotropy, no less valid, nor less empirical, which is diffused through the universe as creation and life. Many glimpses of the universal titanic effort of the forces of light against the darkness have been afforded by historical religions operating at their best, and many unconventional and scattered secular and religious voices presently sound a call for a new religiousness that can use all that the scientific and secular might afford. Under such circumstances, religion need not depend upon its past. It can become a new kind of divine procession into the future.

A NOTE ON SOURCES

If we were to scan all of the written, graphic, and artistic works of mankind prior to the Second World War, we should discover that religion was their chief topic, with political-military subjects a poor second, and commercial records ranking a close third. This fact, significant in itself, daunts whosoever wishes to delve into the literature of religion, or to advise others about doing so.

My direct references are imbedded in the text. To assemble my general sources is an exercise in self-searching that may not profit others. As is the case generally with the humanities and sciences, the ideal reader and critic may have read few of my sources but instead "something else," as good or better, or may have shared few of my experiences that made my sources meaningful, but may have been a keen critic of the language and practices of religion as observed from childhood to old age in his or her own social settings and have read little but thought much, so that he would review his religious materials like Marcel Proust and Thomas Wolfe and James Joyce reworked their lost pasts in their autobiographical novels, making of the past a rich and elegant library.

There are, of course, encyclopaedias about religion and philosophy, and a general encyclopaedia, excepting the Soviet, will offer perhaps a fourth of its articles as entries related to religion. James G. Frazer's *Golden Bough* (13 vols.) is itself an encyclopaedia of the anthropology of religion. Also creations of Robert Graves and Joseph Campbell pertain here.

Almost encyclopaedic, yet entering boldly upon the analytic and systematic, are the studies of Mircea Eliade. His *Patterns in Comparative Religions, The Myth of the Eternal Return, Myth and Reality, Images et Symboles,* and other books are as indispensable as any particular writings can be in an age when hundreds of books and articles descend upon every subject. It may not be too early to alert the reader to the multi-volume encyclopaedia that is being prepared under the editorship of Dr. Eliade through the auspices of Macmillan Publishing Company. [This work is now available]

Every country has had its religious wars, every religion its heretics and apostates, and political history is loaded with religious conflicts. Bibliographies about them can be initially retrieved through encyclopaedias and card catalogues. Too, every sect has its sacred scriptures and polemical masters, readily accessed through its leader's name - Paul, Augustine, Calvin, Wesley, *et al*, as for instance, one proceeds along a particular Protestant Christian line of thought.

Should not one begin with philosophy, to avoid trivia and a waste of time? Would that such were the case. A careless saunter into the woods of theology and philosophy may end up in the oven of a seminarian. Plato is recommended, but not without Aristotle, nor Aquinas without Eckhart, nor Loyola without Kierkegaard, nor Hegel without Marx, and so on.

The sociology of religion seems to me to be continually useful and I am sure that some of the trails of my mind pass through Ludwig Feuerbach, Max Weber, Karl Mannheim, Hans Vaihinger, Benjamin Nelson, and the pragmatists with philosophical links, such as William James and John Dewey. From here it is but a step to the commentators upon science, such as Percy Bridgman and Alfred North Whitehead. In 1873 John W. Draper published *a History of the Conflict of Religion and Science,* but today one seeks out also various works on the conflict of science itself within science. Among the best of these might be Owen Barfield's *Saving the Appearances,* David Bohm's *Causality and Chance in Modern Physics,* D. G. Garan's *The Key to the Sciences of Man,* and Roger S. Jones' *Physics as Metaphor.* Norbert Wiener's famous works on communication science are supplemented by *God and Golem, Inc.: A Comment of Certain Points Where Cybernetics Impinges on Religion.* Roger Shinn and Paul Albrecht have edited a two volume collection on *Faith and Science in an Unjust World.* Among several dozen journals, *Zygon: Journal of Religion and Science,* occurs in this connection. E. A. Shneour and E. A. Olteson have compiled writings and bibliography on *Extraterrestrial Life.*

Psychoanalysis provides a systematic awareness of the unconscious interaction of religious material with the sexual, familial and symbolic. Sigmund Freud's relevant writings are indexed and readily available. One might read Carl Jung more selectively. As in other fields, an occasional perusal of major journals is called for. Most names in this note are of famous men, and fame breeds fame, so that, as here, lesser luminaries are discriminated against erroneously.

Much is made of catastrophe and quantavolution in this work. The reader will have noticed that a background thereto is contained in other books of the author's "Quantavolution Series;" thus, for the physical evidence of quantavolution and disaster, *Chaos and Creation, The Lately Tortured Earth,* and *Solaria Binaria;* for the anthropological and mythological ambiance of religion, *Homo Schizo I, God's Fire,* and *The Disastrous Love Affair of Moon and Mars;* for the psychological, *Homo Schizo II,* as well as the foregoing.

My exposition adopts the format of ordinary language, the structure of whose utterances must be systematic and conventional. Hence the form of communication renders obscure the meanings of mystics, already beset by the problem in their own turn when they write. Such is the case with Meister Eckhart, St. Theresa of Avila, or of Vedanta, Gnosticism, Quakerism, Zen Buddhism, or Sufism; or of the pure symbolists and the occult. Still, laid in the depth psychology of the present work, and concealed by its positivistic style, are paths that a mystic might perhaps follow in exploring the divine within oneself.

Alfred de Grazia was born in 1919 in Chicago and died in 2014 in France. His father, a musician and conductor, had emigrated to the United States from Sicily. Alfred earned his PhD in political science from the University of Chicago. He fought in six campaigns in WWII as one of the first members of the Department of Psychological Warfare at OSS and ended the war as Commanding Officer of the psychological warfare combat propaganda team of the Seventh Army. He taught political science at U. of Minnesota, Brown U., Stanford U., and NYU, and as a guest lecturer in many university in the United States and abroad. He published over twenty books in the field of political science. He created the magazine "The American Behavioral Scientist" and was a pioneer in computerized information retrieval in the social sciences, creating the "Universal Reference System" in the 1960s. He met Immanuel Velikovsky in 1963 and published "The Velikovsky Affair." He created the field of Quantavolution and authored eleven books in the field of catastrophism and ancient history. His 2-million-visitors/y website "www.grazian-archive.com" is another pioneering effort in the field of personal archives. He also wrote poetry, plays and autobiographical works, as well as a three volume History of the United States: "America's History Retold." He created "Kalos Cosmos," a general utopian strategy to achieve a good and just World. He spent his last decades between the United States, France and Greece. He is a member of the French Légion d'Honneur, and a Distinguished Member of the Regiment (DMOR) of Psychological Operations at Fort Bragg, North Carolina.

Michels, Roberto, *First lectures in political sociology*. Translated, with an introduction, by Alfred de Grazia. Minneapolis: University of Minnesota Press, [1949]. And Harper & Row, 1965
Public and republic: political representation in America. New York: Knopf, 1951.
The elements of political science. Series: Borzoi Books in Political Science. New York: Knopf, 1952. And second revised edition: *Politics and government: the elements of political science*. Vol 1: the element of political science and Vol. 2: Political organization. [1962]. New York: Collier, 1962– . And new revised edition, New York: Free Press London: Collier Macmillan, 1965.
The Western Public: 1952 and beyond. [A study of political behaviour in the western United States.]. Stanford: Stanford University Press, [1954.]
The American way of government. National edition. New York : Wiley, [1957]. There is also a "National, State and Local edition". Foundation for Voluntary Welfare.
Grass roots private welfare : winning essays of the 1956 national awards competition of the Foundation for Voluntary Welfare. Alfred de Grazia, editor. New York: New York University Press, 1957.
American welfare. New York: New York University Press, 1961 (with Ted Gurr).
World politics: a study in international relations. Series: College Outline Series. New York: Barnes & Noble, 1962.
Apportionment and representative government. Series: Books that matter. New York : Praeger, c1963
Essay on apportionment and representative government. Washington : American Enterprise Institute, 1963
Revolution in teaching: new theory, technology, and curricula. With an introduction by Jerome Bruner. New York: Bantam Books, [1964] (Editor, with David A. Sohn).
Universal Reference System. *Political science, government, and public policy: an annotated and intensively indexed compilation of significant books, pamphlets, and articles, selected and processed by the Universal Reference System*. Prepared under the direction of Alfred De Grazia, general editor, Carl E. Martinson, managing editor, and John B. Simeone, consultant.

Princeton, N.J.: Princeton Research Pub. Co., 1965–69. *Plus* nine more volumes on the subjects of: *International Affairs; Economic Regulation; Public Policy and the Management of Science; Administrative Management; Comparative Government and Cultures; Legislative Process; Bibliography of Bibliographies in Political Science, Government and Public Policy; Current Events and Problems of Modern Society; Public Opinion, Mass Behavior and Political Psychology; Law, Jurisprudence and Judicial Process.*

Republic in crisis: Congress against the executive force. New York: Federal Legal Publications, [1965].

Political behavior. Series: Elements of political science; 1. New, revised edition. New York: Free press paperback, 1966.

Congress, The First Branch of Government, editor, Doubleday – Anchor Books, 1967

Congress and the Presidency: Their Roles in Modern Times, with Arthur M. Schlesinger, American Enterprise Institute for Public Policy Research, Washington, 1967.

The Behavioral Sciences: Essays in honor of George A. Lundberg, editor, Behavioral Research Council, Great Barrington, Mass;, 1968.

Old Government, New People: Readings for the New politics, et al., Scott, Foresman, Glenview, Ill., 1971.

Politics for Better or Worse, Scott, Foresman, Glenview, Ill., 1973.

Eight Branches of Government: American Government Today, w. Eric Weise, Collegiate Pub., 1975.

Eight Bads – Eight Goods: The American Contradictions, Doubleday – Anchor Books, 1975.

Supporting Art and Culture: 1001 Questions on Policy, Lieber-Atherton, New York, 1979.

A Cloud Over Bhopal: Causes, Consequences, and Constructive Solutions, Kalos Foundation for the India-America Committee for the Bhopal Victims: Popular Prakashan, Bombay, 1985.

The American State of Canaan – the peaceful, prosperous juncture of Israel and Palestine as the 51st State of the United States of America, Metron Publications, Princeton, NJ, 2009

America's History Retold (One)*: Conquest, Colonialism and Constitutions* Metron Publications, Princeton N.J. (1997,2011)

America's History Retold (Two)*: Originating American Ways of Living and Working* Metron Publications, Princeton, N.J. (1997, 2011)

America's History Retold (Three): *Shaping Earth's Cultures and Powers*
Metron Publications, Princeton, N.J. (1997, 2011)

The Quantavolution Series (all with Metron Publications, Princeton, N.J.):

Chaos and Creation, (1981)
God's Fire: Moses and the Management of Exodus, (1982)
The Lately Tortured Earth, (1982)
Homo Schizo I. (1982) New edition: 2014
Homo Schizo II. (1982) New edition: 2015
The Divine Succession, (1982)
The Disastrous Love Affair of Moon and Mars, (1983)
Solaria Binaria, (with E. R. Milton), (1983)
The Burning of Troy, (1984)
Cosmic Heretics, (1984) New edition: 2012
The Iron Age of Mars, (2009)

Biography, Poetry

The Babe, Child of Boom and Bust in Old Chicago, umbilicus mundi, Quiddity
Press, Metron Publications, Princeton, N.J., 1992.
The Student: at Chicago in Hutchin's Hey-day, Quiddity Press, Metron
Publications, Princeton N.J., 1991.
The Taste of War: Soldiering in World War II, Quiddity Press, Metron
Publications, Princeton, N.J., 1992. New edition: Metron
Publications, 2011.
Twentieth Century Fire-Sale, Poetry, Quiddity Press, Metron
Publications, Princeton, N.J., 1996.
A Taste of War - Soldiering in World War II, (revised edition), Metron
Publications, Princeton, NJ, 2011.
The Venus Spy-Trap, Metron Publications, Princeton, N.J., (1989)
Passage of the Year, Poetry, Quiddity Press, Metron publications,
Princeton, N.J., 1967.
Twentieth Century Fire-Sale, Poetry, Quiddity Press, Metron
Publications, Princeton, N.J., 1996.

Films

La Roccia di Sisifo, directed by Pilar Latini, Bergamo, 2004.
Il Gene della Speranza, directed by Kinokitchen, Pisa, 2006.

www.ingramcontent.com/pod-product-compliance
Lightning Source LLC
LaVergne TN
LVHW091256080426
835510LV00007B/278